THE EASTERN FRONT 1914-18

SUICIDE OF THE EMPIRES

THE AUTHOR

Alan Clark is a historian, politician and author. He was member of Parliament for Plymouth Sutton 1974–1992. He stood down from the Commons in 1992 but returned in May 1997 as MP for Kensington & Chelsea. He was Minister for Trade and then No 2 at the Ministry of Defence in Mrs Thatcher's and, latterly, John Major's government.

He enlisted in the Royal Horse Guards in 1945 and in the Royal Auxilliary Air Force from 1951–53. His publications include his bestselling diaries; *The Donkeys* (a history of the British Expeditionary Force in 1915), *The Fall of Crete* and *Barbarossa, The Russian German Conflict 1941–5*. In 1997 he presented a four-part television series – 'The Conservative Party' for BBC-2 and his book *The Tories*, concerning the Nation State 1922–97, was published in 1998.

Other titles in the GREAT BATTLES series

Hastings by Peter Poyntz Wright
Agincourt by Christopher Hibbert
Edgehill 1642 by Peter Young
Marston Moor 1644 by Peter Young
The Boyne and Aughrim: The War of the Two Kings by John Kinross
Trafalgar: The Nelson Touch by David Howarth
Corunna by Christopher Hibbert
Wellington's Peninsular Victories by Michael Glover
Borodino by Digby Smith
Waterloo: A Near Run Thing by David Howarth
Arnhem by Christopher Hibbert

Other Military Books published by the Windrush Press

Letters Home from the Crimea
    Edited by Philip Warner
The Recollections of Rifleman Harris
    Edited and Introduced by Christopher Hibbert
The Letters of Private Wheeler
    Edited and with a Foreword by B. H. Liddell Hart
The Diary of a Napoleonic Foot Soldier
    Edited and Introduced by Marc Raeff
A Soldier of the Seventy-first
    Edited and Introduced by Christopher Hibbert
The Wheatley Diary
    Edited and Introduced by Christopher Hibbert
The Recollections of Sergeant Morris
    Edited by John Selby
The Great Civil War
    By Alfred H. Burne and Peter Young
Capture at Arnhem
    Captain Harry Roberts

THE EASTERN FRONT 1914-18

SUICIDE OF THE EMPIRES

ALAN CLARK

THE WINDRUSH PRESS · GLOUCESTERSHIRE

First published in Great Britain by
BPC in 1971
Reprinted by The Windrush Press in 1999
Little Window, High Street
Moreton-in-Marsh
Gloucestershire GL56 0LL
Tel.: 01608 652012
Fax: 01608 652125
Email: windrush@windrushpress.com

British Library Cataloguing in Publication Data
A catalogue record for this book is available from the British Library

ISBN 1 900624 23 0

Typeset by Archetype IT Ltd, web site http://www.archetype-it.com

Printed and bound in Great Britain by Bell & Bain Ltd., Glasgow

The front cover shows a detail from a painting by Alfred Basel 'The storming of the village
Stary Korczyn by the Landsturminfanterieregiment No. 1 on 22 December 1914' by kind
permission of the Heeresgeschichtliches Museum, Vienna

Cover design by Miranda Harvey

To order your free Windrush Press catalogue featuring all the
titles in the series, plus our travel books, general history and other titles,
please phone us on **01608 652012** or **01608 652025**
Fax us on **01608 652125** Email: **Windrush@Windrushpress.com**
Website: **www.windrushpress.com**
Or write to:
The Windrush Press Limited
Little Window, High Street, Moreton-in-Marsh
Gloucestershire, GL56 0LL, UK

Contents

List of Illustrations, Maps, and Diagrams

CHAPTER THREE

CHAPTER FOUR

MAPS

Prologue

The Delicate Balance

ALTHOUGH WE TEND to think of the 1914–18 war primarily in terms of 'the Western Front' – and rightly, for the social and economic after-effects of the slaughter in Flanders are with us to this day – its origins, and the strategy which governed all but its closing months, lay in the East.

The 'problem' which occupied the three Eastern powers – namely Germany, Austria-Hungary, and Russia – lay in the stresses which afflicted the Habsburg Empire and the threat to its own security which each of the powers believed to be endemic there. France, the fourth European power, felt no territorial threat, but dabbled in Eastern politics with the object of tying down Germany against whom she had the unsettled score of defeat in the Franco-Prussian War of 1870.

The Habsburg Empire was an irregular hotchpotch of homogeneous nationalities, without natural frontiers, or any unifying economic structure. The result of a settlement made in 1867, it reflected the old feudal concepts of allegiance owed by serfs to their lord, and ignored, indeed reacted against the 'revolutionary' doctrine of nationality which had originally been aroused by Napoleon I and had erupted periodically thereafter.

But the more ramshackle and insecure the Habsburg structure became, the more essential did its preservation appear to the 'stability' of the area. The Prussians had inflicted a sharp military defeat on the Austrians at Königgrätz in 1866 and thus ended Habsburg dreams of dominating the affairs of Germany (at that time still divided into several independent states). From then on, and especially after the setting up of the German Empire under their domination in 1871, the Prussians devoted their diplomatic energies and their economic largesse to bolstering up the Habsburg Empire, which offered a substantial 'buffer' against the encroachments of Russia on their own southern flank. This was especially clear after the alliance between France and Russia in 1893.

The prime source of weakness of the Austrian Empire was the large Slav population which felt its allegiances steadily drawn towards the

Empire's various independent neighbours to the south and east and, particularly, towards Serbia. By 1913 effective political unity was felt to be threatened. An enormous and ramshackle secret police pervaded the whole machine, from whose civil service the dissident nationalities were first excluded, then, as part of 'concessions', embraced. Serbs, Croats, Transylvanians, and Czechs alternately conspired with and against the Austrians and the Hungarians for positions in the army and the administration. Yet in contrast to its Balkan neighbours the Austro-Hungarian Empire remained – at an administrative level – relatively stable.

At the turn of the century the techniques of 'resistance' as we know them today were in their infancy. Sheer force of arms might have kept

1   Russian Cossacks assembling for patrol

the Empire together for another fifty years if it had not been for the military threat, and the diplomatic activities of Tsarist Russia, the greatest Slav power. These were neither open nor co-ordinated, and sprang from a mixture of brotherly Slav sentiment and vague territorial and strategic ambitions in the Balkans and against Turkey. But they were enough to give the revolutionaries hope and to cause both the Austrians and the Germans anxiety.

The Germans shared a common frontier of over 400 miles with Russia, or rather with Russian Poland. It was from Russia that the German General Staff saw the main and growing threat to their security. The deterioration of Austrian strength, the removal of its large (if inefficient) army from the German southern flank, and its substitution by a series of unreliable Balkan states under Russian influence, threatened to undermine the Empire.

The second factor which exercised the German General Staff was the danger of a French attack to recover the provinces of Alsace and Lorraine ceded in 1871, which would almost certainly be simultaneous with any outbreak in the East. The French for their part realised that they could never again stand alone against the German army and that it was not simply the recovery of Alsace but their own military survival that depended on a Russian involvement with Germany in the East. This involvement could itself be most easily contrived by threats to the integrity of the Habsburg Empire. Hence a delicate and intricate system of balanced alliances and commitments between these four European great powers ensured that if anything went wrong it was likely that the outbreak of war would involve all of them.

2   The great enigma – the Tsar and his formidable forces. Tsar Nicholas II in the centre of Red Square celebrating the 300th Anniversary of the Romanov Dynasty, 24 May 1913

1

The Armies of the Tsar

FOLLOWING on the defeat of Napoleon in 1815 the Russian armies were the most formidable in the world. They dominated the peace conference and stood ready, or so it was widely believed, as again in 1945, to sweep across and subjugate the continent of Europe.

For nearly a century military technology advanced very little. Vast masses of men remained all-important, the key to victory. And those new inventions, the machine-gun and the high-explosive shell, seemed by the very scale on which they could inflict casualties to underline the importance of numerical superiority.

Experience in the Crimea, and later in the war against Japan had shown that although the Russian armies could be defeated in local battles, their numbers and the vast spaces of their homeland made it impossible for any lesser power to inflict an irredeemable strategic defeat. A familiar theory of historic stalemate revived – that the Russians were invincible in defence, but not formidably aggressive. Then a new development threatened to give the Russian mass tremendous leverage and power – the speed with which the railway could endow a manoeuvring army added a wholly new dimension to military mobility. For the first time in the history of war armies could assemble, and alter direction, at a speed faster than a man's walk. And how much faster! In the German autumn manoeuvres of 1912 General Helmuth von Moltke had switched three corps from his left to his right flank in an afternoon. The daily radius of a division's striking power, reckoned for five hundred years at 30 miles, seemed now without limit and, still more important, so did the density into which they could concentrate.

All this was not lost on those indefatigable students of military theory, the German General Staff. The superior training and equipment of their own troops was now gravely threatened: first, by a concentration at the point of enemy attack (*schwerpunkt*) so massive that no line could hold against it; secondly, by the speed with which a breakthrough could be reinforced and exploited.

The General Staff accordingly urged, and secured, an intensive development of the domestic railway system, especially in East Prussia. They also evolved two alternative plans for defeating their traditional enemy – both of them highly perilous. The first entailed an immediate attack with their own front-line strength, with the intention of defeating the Russian standing army in position, thus so dislocating their military machine that the enormous mobilisation which the railways had now so hideously accelerated could never gather momentum; this involved the risk of a dangerously deep penetration of the Russian homeland without strategic result.

The second was to use the full German strength in the West at the outset, relying on the three- to four-week respite which they could expect from the start to completion of the Russian mobilisation schedule. This came to be adopted, purportedly on purely strategic grounds – more likely because a single-minded genius, Schlieffen, had perfected his plan for the right wheel on Paris to the exclusion of all other detailed study. When he died it was both accepted and codified *in perpetuo*. It had built into it a highly dangerous fuse effect which was that the railway layout (and principally the constriction of the trunk lines in Aachen) made it almost impossible to reverse the initial mobilisation measures once they had been set in motion. To this extent Germany (and Germany alone) was committed to war once she was committed to mobilisation, for mobilisation itself had come to mean an exclusive commitment to the Schlieffen Plan.

If mass was indeed the key to victory, then Russian strength was truly formidable. Out of a population of nearly 170,000,000 the Tsar had a standing army of 1,423,000, a large number of which were inevitably deployed in the East and in Central Asia. Equivalent German strength was 856,000 which would itself have to be divided – in whatever proportion the chosen plan dictated – between the Western and Eastern fronts.

Mobilisation would boost the German figure to nearer 4,000,000 but (for the Germans in particular) it was a highly complex and critical operation that tended to dislocate, and thus gravely impair, the fighting efficiency of the army until it was completed. The more leisurely Russian pace involved bringing 3,000,000 men to the colours in their first stage with a further 3,500,000 to follow and – in theory at least – to be under arms within three months of the outbreak of war.

Yet it was the virtual parity between these two figures – which could

3 & 4 The Russian 'steam-roller' on display. Its numbers disguised weakness. The cavalry (top) was more concerned with display rather than with tactical skill. The artillery though (bottom) was well-equipped but ill-organised

5 Prince Leopold von Bayern inspects the troops early in the war before the shrapnel helmet, the 'coal-skuttle', had been adopted

6 German heavy artillery was much superior

only co-exist for a critical eight to ten weeks between the completion of the German mobilisation and the start of the Russian second stage – that haunted the General Staff planning. It seemed inconceivable that the war could last more than three months, and inevitable that some decision would be arrived at within that period, as it had in the Franco-Prussian and in the Austro-Prussian Wars.

THE VITAL DIFFERENCES

But in fact numbers formed only a part of the calculus – and a much smaller part than was generally accepted. The German standing army was virtually uniform in quality and training; the quality of the Russian army was highly variable. The German plans were backed by a logistics system whose functioning had been worked out to the smallest detail; the Russians expected to fight with the supplies they carried and then to 'live off the land' (an assumption which, in relation to ammunition demands at least, was highly perilous).

The German artillery was a homogeneous force, with the new 77-mm field piece distributed down to battalion level; the Russian artillery was largely autonomous: above divisional level it functioned under an independent chain of command and much of its equipment was over fifty years old. It was backed by a private civil service – the Artillery Department at the Ministry of War – which arranged its budgeting and procurement.

At the outbreak of war there were sixty heavy batteries in the Russian army, compared with 381 in that of the Germans. Despite the fact that the Russians deployed an 8-gun battery, against the 6-gun battery used by the Germans – increasing their strength to the equivalent of eighty German batteries – German fire-power was much superior. The Russian Division had seven light batteries attached, the (smaller) German Division had fourteen. Each Russian corps had only one light howitzer battery.

Bombardment from the air was not a factor in 1914, but reconnaissance and artillery spotting were already important. At the start of hostilities there were 129 Russian pilots and 100 observers. But for 1914 *Jane's All the World's Aircraft* lists (by name) 184 German military 'aviators' with a further 315 names described as 'private, but available for war duties'. In terms of equipment the Russian line-up was of moderate quality – a few Farman 'pushers', some Aviatik and Nieuport two-seaters built under licence, and 13 non-rigid Dirigibles. In fact all the Nieuports had a built-in wing defect which made them dangerous in operations and lethal for training. Logistics backing was negligible, with the total engine output of the Gnome factory (making French Gnome-Rhône engines) at five units per month. Against this the Germans could field large numbers of Albatross and, later, of Fokkers, Taubes, and biplanes of greatly superior performance, operating from regular and established flying fields at Allenstein, Insterburg, and Königsberg.

In the Baltic the familiar picture of Russian qualitative inferiority was not lightened by any numerical preponderance. For the Germans could at any time feed ships through the Kiel Canal out of the High Seas Fleet. There were four 12-inch-gun battle-cruisers (designed on Clydebank) building but only one was near completion in 1914. Neither they nor the ill-fated *Slava*-class battleships (of which five had been sunk by the Japanese in the war of 1905) were any match for the 12-inch *Helgoland* or 11-inch *Westfallen* classes which opposed them. The Russians had been slow in developing torpedo-boats and destroyers and their naval strategy was strictly defensive, closing the Gulf of Kronstadt with mines and shore batteries.

The fact that the German Services maintained a system of promotion by merit was another significant point of difference between these two great armies. The Russian army, it is true, possessed a number of able and energetic officers but there was also much dead wood – social dropouts, failed landowners, placemen of every kind and, in the higher echelons, court favourites. Many of the elite cavalry regiments were superb on the parade ground, but they suffered from a kind of introspective rivalry that paid more attention to *dressage* and the splendour of the men's uniforms (often largely paid for out of the commander's purse – or more likely the commander's credit with a Jewish money-lender in Vilna or Lemberg) than to tactical combat skills.

The Russian army reflected the qualities, divisions, and corruptions of society itself. In 1914 there were some 30,000 leading families who controlled the countryside and, therefore, the economy. Some of these families held estates so vast that they could ride on horseback for a week without leaving their own land. Total freehold estates amounted to some 2,000,000,000 acres. The *moujhiks*, labourers on these properties, formed

The situation on the eve of war showing the rival alliances and their armed forces before and after mobilisation

7   The Russian officer corps in action. Individual officers were energetic, but the system encouraged sloth and indolence

the rank and file of the conscript armies. The NCOs were drawn from the 10,000,000 small-holders who eked out an existence on the fringes of large estates. The cruel climate and the dismal hardships of life so close to the soil bred a special kind of soldier, hardy, stoic, brave but without initiative and, inevitably, illiterate. Even among the NCOs there were few who could read or write and the commoner military signs and identifications were recognised only by their familiarity. Orders were given verbally.

General Danilov writes of the defeatism and breakdown of order among these forces even early in the war:

> During the solemn session of the Duma, the President forbade a deputy of the Left to deliver his speech, judging it too defeatist . . . At the beginning of mobilisation disorders occurred in many places among reserve units. Sometimes, as in Barnaul, they were quite serious, and had to be repressed forcibly, even by the use of arms.
>
> The current explanation advanced for the disorders, drunkenness, is not satisfactory, because an imperial order had forbidden the sale of liquor. Rather, a deep ferment of disintegration was already pervading the masses. The crowds of reservists were driven by an evil spirit, inciting them to plunder and create disorder. Even at St Petersburg people's initial enthusiasm eventually turned into monstrous, unruly demonstrations. In the evening of 4th August I witnessed scenes of depravity caused by outbreaks of the baser instincts of the crowds. The Russian people was psychologically unprepared for war. The large masses of peasants did not fully understand why they were called up to arms. The *moujhik* went to war because he was accustomed to complying with any order given him by the authorities. Passive and patient, he was used to bearing his cross till the time of great trials.

Despite this predominantly feudal social structure, the beginnings of a new meritocracy were everywhere to be seen. In the first decade of the century, stimulated by the war with Japan, brought in by French entrepreneurs or filtering eastwards from Austria and Prussia, the seeds of industry – chemicals and electrical engineering, metallurgy, textiles, and oil – had taken root. Someone had to run these new industries and it was a task to which the landowning families were neither inclined nor suited. Instead, the recruits came from the expanding middle class of town-dwellers, merchants, and shopkeepers, and the children of civil servants.

Although this new class disposed of administrative power (of a kind) it was resolutely excluded from the realm of political influence. 'Intelligentsia,' said the Tsar, 'how I detest that word! I wish I could order the Academy to strike it from the Russian dictionary.' The Duma, a kind of mock Parliament which had been forced on the Tsar following the revolution of 1905, was virtually ignored and the day-to-day running of the country was in the hands of the *Tchinovniki*, a body of senior administrators drawn from the nobility and inevitably influenced by court favourites and hangers-on with social or monetary power.

Efficiency – particularly military efficiency – suffered badly. Senior officers were never retired, but hung about the barracks gambling and drawing full pay. The Staff College was filled with idle young aristocrats who used it as a hall of residence from which to raid the flesh-pots of St Petersburg. As late as 1916, the Staff Office was completely closed *fifteen times* in May for 'public holidays'.

THE CONFLICT OF TALENTS

The conflict of talents in the Tsarist army can best be illustrated by comparing the two men at the top: Grand Duke Nicholas, the Commander-in-Chief and uncle of the Tsar, and General Sukhomlinov, the Minister of War. The Grand Duke stood six foot six and was (for that epoch) exceptionally slim. He had played a creditable part in bringing about the constitutional reforms of 1905 – and earned much resentment at Court for so doing. As Inspector-General of Cavalry in the Russo-Japanese War he had acquired operational experience without bearing personal responsibility for defeat in battle: later he had been appointed to the presidency of the Council of National Defence. With his pointed beard, pale blue eyes, and commanding stature the Grand Duke was a standing example of what a 'real' Tsar should look and behave like. It was hardly surprising that the bored and lethargic Nicholas II should feel uneasy in his uncle's presence, that the Court should intrigue against and the Tsarina detest him.

General Sukhomlinov was the palace favourite:

> He was short and soft with a cat-like face, neat white whiskers and beard, and an ingratiating, almost feline manner that captivated those whom he set himself to please. In others he inspired distrust at first sight. Ministerial office, both appointment and dismissal, being entirely at the whim of the Tsar, Sukhomlinov had won and kept himself in favour by being at once obsequious and entertaining, by funny stories and acts of buffoonery, avoidance of serious and unpleasant matters . . .

8   A group of Russian officers

9   Grand Duke Nicholas, the commander-in-chief of the Russian army and uncle to the Tsar

10   General Sukhomlinov (left of picture) with his chief-of-staff, General Janushkevich

There is a contemporary photograph of Sukhomlinov, walking in full panoply with his chief-of-staff, General Janushkevich. It is evident from the shine on their thigh boots that they have only just dismounted, but already Sukhomlinov has the appearance of being short of breath and the pouchiness around his eyes reminds one of the French Ambassador's acid comment that 'he was keeping all his energies for conjugal pleasures with a wife thirty-two years younger than himself'. Nor does the appearance of General Janushkevich fit well with the image of a chief-of-staff (he was the fifth to fill the post in as many years). Only forty-four years old, he had gone straight to the Staff College without regimental experience, though he had later served briefly in the same Guards unit as Nicholas II. He has the waxed moustache, curly black hair, and wary, deferential manner of the professional courtier.

Yet if the leadership was largely corrupt and incompetent, the Russian army could nonetheless turn out a formidable review each year to impress the foreign attachés. It was a 'steam-roller'. Slow, perhaps, to get under way, but unstoppable once it had gathered momentum. The enigma of its performance was one of the foremost problems in every German or Habsburg 'war game'. To the French, however, whose generals were wedded to the doctrine of the offensive, and convinced that 'vigour and tenacity are more important than tactical skill', it was of vital importance. Despite their beliefs, the generals perceived quite clearly that their own projected attack in Alsace and Lorraine – the clumsy and unimaginative Plan 17 – would face hopeless odds unless a sizable proportion of the German army were diverted to the East. The danger period lay in that overlong interval between the Russian declaration of war and the completion of mobilisation. The diplomatic, military, and economic energies of the French Embassy in St Petersburg were accordingly devoted single-mindedly to preserving France from danger.

The ambassador, Maurice Paléologue (from whose diaries we derive much information on the intrigues of the Tsarist Court), had a good deal running in his favour. French was the official language of the Court; Paris was a social mecca, where much of the aristocracy journeyed every summer, and where their daughters went to finishing schools; French military prowess and theory – for some unaccountable reason – were greatly admired, although the Russians would have done better to ignore it and study instead the lessons of their own more recent experience in battle, against Japan.

Staff talks, at the highest level, were held every year between the two

countries. The Tsar agreed that he would order an offensive simultaneously with the French attack in the West, or not later than the sixteenth
day after mobilisation, with whatever troops were to hand. And in return
the French made substantial grants from their exchequer towards
equipping the Russian army and improving its communications.

Some figures will show just how serious a handicap to the mobility of
her army was Russia's inadequate railway system. In Germany there were
10.6 miles of track per 100 square miles of territory – in Russia, only one.
The average distance to be covered by rail by a Russian recruit, from
entrainment point to mobilisation centre was 600–700 miles, in France
or Germany it was 160 miles. There were six double-track lines and two
single-track lines from the Petrograd meridian to the zones of concentration, but lateral movement (i.e. from one front to another) was quite
undeveloped. Consequently rolling stock in any one theatre was
effectively stuck there for the duration of a campaign. The freight cars
were not equipped with automatic brakes (to do so required a grant of
20,000,000 roubles, which was never voted). Even within their own
theatres, that is operating radially, the average maximum daily mileage of
a troop train was 200 compared with 400 in France or Germany.

It is doubtful how much of the money contributed by France was

11   Russian infantry; hard, stoic, but short of ammunition

actually applied to its intended purpose. A celebrated story recounts how a French businessman, seeking a contract to supply 10,000 platoon tents, was duly placing his bribes in the Ministry of War. Finally he came to the highest point, the minister's personal secretary, in whose chamber the order would be signed. To the businessman's alarm the private secretary insisted on a personal 'gratuity' equal in size to all the lesser disbursements which he had been obliged to make on the way up. He protested that, if this last sum were paid out he would have no profit left on the order. 'Ah,' replied the secretary with a silky smile, 'I understand. But why deliver the tents?'

It was a highly wasteful process. The inefficiency and corruption of the Russian governmental machine ensured that there was little likelihood of a *successful* campaign at such short notice. But to the French it was not a success on the battlefield which mattered. Indeed they would probably (like the West in the Second World War) have preferred a stalemate there. What was essential was that a start, a move of some kind however unproductive, should be made in those opening weeks. Of one commodity – blood – the Tsar disposed an apparently inexhaustible supply. If he should expend enough, and fast enough, the French believed that this might allow them victory in the West.

12 Russian reserves are called up. Their commander-in-chief was 'filled with pessimism' at the prospect of going into action

2

Tannenberg

FOLLOWING the assassination of the Archduke Franz Ferdinand and his wife on 28th June 1914, and the subsequent declarations of war – by Austria-Hungary (on Serbia), Germany (on both France and Russia), and Great Britain and Belgium (on Germany) – the stage was set for the opening of the war.

The Eastern campaign required fighting of a kind very different from the sodden trench lines of Flanders or the terrible siege perimeters of Verdun. In the West no more set-piece battles were fought after the Marne, but in the East positional warfare was a last resort, forced on the combatants by mutual exhaustion or the hostility of the season. But the same sad human characteristics are common to both theatres – the mindless bravery and devotion of the men, and the mulish obstinacy and ignorance of the commanders who sacrificed them.

It was the Germans, with their excellent equipment and intelligent leadership who dominated the battlefield, even when outnumbered. The Russian and the Habsburg armies moved across a truly Napoleonic canvas: huge masses of cavalry screened their flanks or cantered outriding in the van; dense-packed columns of infantry and 'baggage' raised the dust under the naked eye of their enemy whose poor gunnery, shortage of ammunition, or plain stupidity often allowed such manoeuvres to go unpunished.

During the first encounter in East Prussia in August 1914, the German advantages were at a discount. The Russians were fresh, and their magazines full. Nor did the Germans enjoy their customary advantage of superior leadership. General von Prittwitz, commander of VIII Army, whose three corps were responsible for defending East Prussia during the critical opening weeks – while the Schlieffen Plan brought France to her knees – was a man whose main interest seems to have been not military affairs or even their sporting ancillaries such as riding, swordsmanship, or display, but . . . food. Known (within earshot though not actually to his face) as *der Dicke* ('fatso'), he was a man of excessive corpulence even during an epoch when girth was reckoned as a sign of respectability. Prittwitz was sixty-seven years old in 1914; he was a court favourite of long standing with a good line in mess-room stories and had proved well-connected enough to resist at least two attempts by Moltke – who was well aware of the strategic importance of the VIII Army command – to have him removed.

Moltke's fears for the fate of the VIII Army found, perhaps, reflection in his orders to it. He expressly forbade Prittwitz to seek security by withdrawal into the Königsberg fortress network; then somewhat vaguely said that the army 'must not allow itself to be overwhelmed by superior forces'. If it 'found itself threatened' by these greatly superior forces, it was to withdraw behind the Vistula.

13   General Sukhomlinov reads a German newspaper

14   An endless line of Russian troops on the march

The deputy chief-of-operations at VIII Army was a Colonel Max Hoffmann, and much more will be heard of him in these pages. Like Prittwitz, he was fat; unlike his commander, Hoffmann was highly intelligent, and possessed a keen eye for tactical opportunity (as also for human weakness). Hoffmann's verdict on Moltke's contingency orders for VIII Army was that they contained 'psychological dangers' (i.e. temptations) for 'weak characters'. The question remained – how capable were the Russians of forcing the issue when war broke out?

The Russian chain of command was cumbersome in the extreme, and weak in several of its links. At the top stood Sukhomlinov and the Grand Duke Nicholas, each detesting the other, avoiding contact except where formally necessary, and each complaining – the Grand Duke stiltedly, Sukhomlinov archly – to the Tsar. Below the Grand Duke was a long-serving staff officer, lately promoted to active command, General Jilinsky. Jilinsky had been chief-of-staff to the commander-in-chief in the war against Japan, then moved to St Petersburg as Janushkevich's predecessor in which post he had conducted staff talks in Paris concerning the projected Russian operations. Following these talks the Russian plan had been put to the test in the autumn manoeuvres of 1913 and Jilinsky had pronounced himself as 'filled with pessimism' as to the outcome. Yet now, paradoxically, as commander of the North-Western Army Group he found himself charged with putting it into execution.

The plan was an exceedingly obvious one, a giant pincer movement between the Russian 1st and 2nd Armies – the 'Vilna' and 'Warsaw' armies as the Germans called them (the German Staff identifying them from their major entraining points). In fact these two armies, 1st under General Rennenkampf, 2nd under General Samsonov, were too far apart to give one another mutual support at the outset and, even if ideal schedules of advance were maintained, unlikely to be close enough to threaten a real squeeze until about fifteen days after their advance began. It was, too, especially important that Rennenkampf and Samsonov should keep in step, so that the pressure they exerted might be uniform. In the 1913 manoeuvres, and also in the 'war games' played with the same cast in April of 1914, it was apparent that Rennenkampf went too fast. This had been foreseen, with his usual clarity of vision as long ago as 1909 by Schlieffen who had briefly taken time off from his obsession with the Western Front to advise 'Strike with all possible strength at the first Russian army that comes within reach!' (See map, p 31.)

Yet Sukhomlinov, who had played the part of commander-in-chief at the 'war games', had done nothing to alter the schedule. Indeed the importance of speed was urged, indiscriminately, on all the participants. The Tsar felt his personal prestige to be at stake – he had given his bond to the French – and if professional military opinion was united on one point, it was this conviction that the issue had to be forced against the German army before it could be reinforced from the West.

THE FIRST CLASHES

Predictably, then, it was Rennenkampf's 1st Army which came into action first. On 12th August one of his cavalry divisions brushed aside a thin German screen and broke into the town of Margrabowa which they sacked. General Gourko, the commander, justified his action on the grounds that the men's indignation had been aroused by finding that a number of women who had been rounded up for 'pleasure' contained a quorum of German sharp-shooters disguised in skirts!

For the next four days Rennenkampf gradually widened his front, bringing additional divisions and artillery into action while his cavalry galloped at random across the countryside terrorising the farms and villages. The German army was nowhere to be seen.

To the south-west, almost 100 miles distant, Samsonov's columns trudged patiently in the direction of the enemy. The heat was stifling. The roads, narrow sandy tracks through pine forests, soon collapsed under the weight of men and wagons, enforcing prolonged halts while logs were cut and laid, and horses limbered up in tandem to haul guns and limbers from out of the soft dust. A week after the start Samsonov's army was spread out over miles of virtually uninhabited dried marsh and woodland. A dense parched column of march, suspended, it must have seemed, in a limbo of heat and white dust, cut off from the enemy and even – save for periodic messages to make haste – from its own HQ.

But to the Germans, and Prittwitz in particular, the passing of each day was loaded with menace. Of course he should follow Schlieffen's edict and tackle the Russian armies singly. But might this not involve a contravention of Moltke's later orders, that he should avoid being 'overwhelmed'? Certainly the enemy was immeasurably superior: that in

15   'Cossacks at work'. A German propaganda postcard

16   German troops watching for movement

itself, Prittwitz believed, was half-way to giving him licence to withdraw behind the Vistula.

The German staff had rightly anticipated that Rennenkampf would be the first to give battle, and a position had been prepared, on ground of their own choosing, at Gumbinnen. Colonel Hoffmann had arranged that the three regular corps and half the reserve corps should be concentrated here, where they could fall on Rennenkampf at the very moment when he would be feeling the drag on his communications. Then, having checked Rennenkampf, the three corps could be switched south-east to confront Samsonov. Unfortunately for Hoffmann's plan, and Prittwitz's dignity, the leading I Corps, under the command of General von François, was recruited entirely from East Prussians highly resentful of any plan which involved their tamely surrendering the Fatherland to the Slav. On 16th August François had already advanced beyond the Gumbinnen position and had his cavalry in contact with Rennenkampf. On being told over the telephone to halt, François, somewhat impertinently, replied that ' . . . the nearer to Russia I engage the enemy, the less the risk to German territory'.

This was ridiculous. But what was Prittwitz to do? He could hardly relieve a victorious and dashing corps commander in the field. That night he sent François a reprimand, repeating his order not to advance further and reminding his subordinate that he was 'the sole commander'.

On the following day, 17th August, a heavy lunch at VIII Army HQ at Bartenstein was interrupted by further news from I Corps. Triumphantly, François announced his arrival at Stallupönen, an advance of a further 20 miles! Prittwitz was furious. Such disobedience was unparalleled in the German army. There were grave tactical objections, also, as Hoffmann reminded him. If battle were joined too far east of the Gumbinnen position it might well prove indecisive while all the time the 'Warsaw' army was closing the distance in the south. Prittwitz broke off the meal. He drafted a peremptory note ordering an 'immediate retirement' to Gumbinnen, and despatched it by hand of a major-general.

However, by the time the emissary arrived at Stallupönen battle had already been joined. François, more by luck than skill, had cornered two brigades of Russian troops without their artillery, and sensing victory he returned the startled major-general to HQ with the message: 'Inform General von Prittwitz that General von François will break off the engagement when he has defeated the Russians!'

That evening, with 3,000 prisoners under guard, François was on the way back to the lines of Gumbinnen. The Russians were making no attempt to follow. It was plain that they had been given a 'bloody nose' and Prittwitz forgot, or affected to forget, his subordinate's insolence.

François, however, was cock-a-hoop. He saw himself as the saviour of East Prussia – a posture which was sedulously cultivated not only by his staff, but by all those local dignitaries and officials from the threatened territories who clustered about his HQ. At mid-day on the 19th François telephoned to Prittwitz and held forth on the great opportunities for gaining further advantage; he enlarged too, on the plight of the inhabitants, on the shame to German arms of a continuing retreat, and so forth.

Prittwitz was uneasy. Tactically, as Hoffmann reminded him, it was essential that the Russians be lured into the ambush on the western side of Gumbinnen, indeed, left to himself, Prittwitz would have preferred going back all the way to the Vistula or, better still, into the fastnesses of

17   Russian prisoners under guard

Königsberg. But it made a poor impression. As a practised retailer of Court gossip Prittwitz well knew that rumours of cowardice were fatal at the Palace. Then, in the late afternoon, an intercepted message from Rennenkampf to his corps commanders confirmed that the Russians had been halted.

Barely had this message been decoded (the Russians were using a simple block code which had been broken at the outset of the campaign by a mathematics professor attached to VIII Army HQ) when a second one was brought to Prittwitz of still greater importance. It was from the commander of the solitary and depleted German XX Corps to the south, and reported that Samsonov's army was beginning to emerge from the barren pine dunes of northern Poland and to cross the boundaries of Prussia. Now it was plain that the carefully sited positions along the River Angerapp, where Hoffmann had planned to trap Rennenkampf as he emerged from Gumbinnen, would never be used. The VIII Army must either step forward now, and smash Rennenkampf, or it must withdraw another 40 miles, wheeling in the process, to turn and confront Samsonov.

Galvanised, Prittwitz issued his orders. Certainly François was to attack; he was to attack immediately, that is, at dawn the next day; and so was

Mackensen with the XVIII Corps (Mackensen had been obediently waiting at the Angerapp); as was the I Reserve Corps under General Otto von Below.

There was no time to co-ordinate a plan of attack or, indeed, to ensure that the operation took place simultaneously on all three corps frontages. Coming as the culmination of twenty years of manoeuvres and 'war games' this first attempt to conform with Schlieffen's advice was launched with a degree of spontaneity and improvisation of which a local company commander might well have been ashamed.

INITIAL GERMAN DEFEAT

As was to be expected, François was first into action. Advancing in the half light, following a dawn bombardment, his men suffered grievously from the Russian guns until these ran out of ammunition. By mid-day he was at grips with the Russian infantry and had forced his cavalry and some light horse artillery round in a wide sweep where they fell on the Russian baggage train. But without support on his flanks François did not dare push his corps any deeper into the Russian mass – and such support as he might have expected was already withering. Mackensen's XVIII Corps had been badly delayed by crowds of refugees and their livestock who were congesting the bridges on the Angerapp. Exhausted by an all-night march the Germans found themselves under heavy fire as the sun rose before they had even deployed for attack. Being opposite Rennenkampf's centre the XVIII Corps took the full weight of his heavy artillery and in the afternoon, when the first detachments of white-bloused Russian infantry began to counterattack, the whole corps started to disintegrate. Mackensen and his staff drove frenziedly back and forth in their 50-hp Daimler exhorting the men to stand fast, but to no avail. Most of the XVIII was back on its starting line by the mid-afternoon, the demoralised soldiers having, at its southern extremity, brushed with the patiently advancing men of Prittwitz's third and last corps, Below's I Reserve.

Below was heading for collision with the Russians at their strongest point, on the edge of the Rominten forest, and had given prolonged warning of his approach. Indeed, by the time his men were in action the issue of the main battle was already decided, for François had his flank dangerously exposed by Mackensen's precipitate retreat in the centre and found his own local success nullified. During two hours of confused fighting and under heavy fire the German soldiers gradually shuffled northwards so as to cover Mackensen's retreat, but there was no chance of them making contact with François. At 5 o'clock Below broke off the action and he, too, began to march west. The battle of Gumbinnen was over, and Schlieffen's essential prerequisite – that the first Russian army to come within reach should be ruthlessly struck down – had proved impossible.

Back at HQ the heat on that August evening was stifling; clouds of midges swirled in the garden where the staff officers gravely paced up and down, and invaded the map-room, where Prittwitz slumped in an enormous leather armchair, soaked in perspiration. In his memoirs Hoffmann has recorded that the commander ' . . . had for the moment lost command of his nerves'.

With the dusk came still more ominous news. General von Scholtz, who had sole responsibility for the southern front with the depleted XX Corps, reported that Samsonov's 'Warsaw' army was now across the border in strength, that 'four or five corps are advancing over a front 50 to 60 miles wide'. That settled it. Prittwitz, who had already decided – with some satisfaction, it may be thought – to retreat to the Vistula, now made up his mind that it would not be safe to stop even there. At that time of year the river was low; it offered little obstacle to the enemy. Prittwitz's first concern, he told his staff (whom he had summoned indoors on receiving Scholtz's bulletin) was to keep his army 'in being'.

Hoffmann protested. The chief-of-operations showed with a geometric compass that such a retreat was impossible . . . . 'Samsonov is nearer to the Vistula than we are ourselves . . . .' Prittwitz insisted that his orders were obeyed. Somewhat insolently and mindful (perhaps) of the insubordination which François had shown the previous evening, Hoffmann asked to be 'instructed' on the execution of a manoeuvre which was geographically impossible.

The scene was cut short by the telephone. It was Moltke at Coblenz, to whom Prittwitz had booked a call so as to inform him of his decision.

The conversation between these two, on that evening of 20th August, had two direct consequences both of critical importance in deciding the course – and indeed the outcome – of the war. Moltke, who had a low opinion of Prittwitz anyway, decided to sack him. The men he replaced him with were to fight the most successful annihilation battle of the First World War. But still more important, the evident gravity of the situation in the East caused Moltke to order, forthwith, the detachment of three

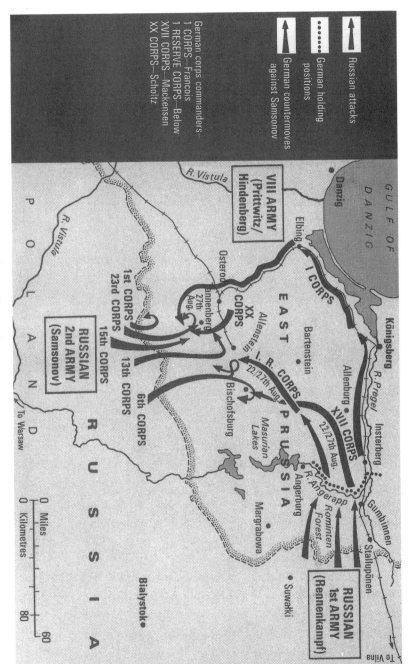

The battlefield of Tannenberg showing the German trap

corps and a cavalry division from Belgium, to be entrained for East Prussia. This weakening of the right wing, where Schlieffen had begged on his death-bed that every last man be deployed, would be regretted bitterly by the Germans in September. At a moment of desperate military crisis – and by no means for the last time in the war – pressure of events in the East was to save the French army from extinction.

More than 50 miles to the south-west of Prittwitz's anxious HQ, Samsonov was driving his men forward. The Russians marched more than twelve hours a day, there was never enough food for soldiers or horses, often at evening they could not even find enough to drink. Already the whole army was half exhausted and in some confusion with many units separated from their artillery, or their supplies, and their horses double-harnessed on the limbers.

Miraculously, Samsonov was keeping to the schedule laid down in the plan – which had always eluded him in the 'war games', yet Jilinsky continued to assume that he was not and showered him with recriminatory telegrams urging haste. To no effect Samsonov replied that he was ' . . . advancing according to time-table'. Jilinsky, with whom communications were highly imperfect, insisted on ' . . . immediate and decisive operations'.

'The great weariness of my men,' Samsonov reported on 22nd August, 'makes a higher speed impossible. The country is devastated, the horses have long been without oats, there is no bread.' Yet in spite of this, Samsonov had achieved prodigies of manoeuvre. By 25th August he had deployed all five corps in line of battle. The 'Iron Corps' – the 15th of General Martos – stood in the centre, while the cavalry probed far to the north through the swampy hinterland of the Masurian Lakes, searching in vain for Rennenkampf's left wing.

The whole essence of the Russian plan consisted in the joint, and convergent, pressure of the two widely separate wings. It was always assumed that the southern pincer was that which would lag behind schedule, for the eastern arm had a shorter distance to travel, and an easier route, and this assumption had twice been borne out in manoeuvres. Yet now, in action, it was Samsonov who was ahead and Rennenkampf who dawdled.

After the Russian victory at Gumbinnen, Rennenkampf made no effort to pursue. On the evening of battle he had told his staff, 'You can take off your clothes now . . . [and go to bed] . . . the Germans are retiring.' The days passed, and still Rennenkampf hardly moved. No one bothered

18   Russian troops going 'over-the-top', East Prussia in 1914

him; all the telegrams went to Samsonov. The effect on the grand tactics of the campaign was little different from that which would have followed his defeat at Gumbinnen instead of the German repulse which had actually taken place.

THE NEW TEAM

The significance of this was not lost at the HQ of the German VIII Army, where the panic of 20th August had fast evaporated. Moltke, on the 21st, had individually telephoned to the various corps commanders and found, in conversation with them, that the situation, and the prospects were not as bad as Prittwitz painted. Prittwitz himself walked into the trap that afternoon by ringing Moltke again and complaining about his staff and their plan to turn on the 'Warsaw' army as being 'too daring'. That settled it. Still moving at breakneck pace Moltke dismissed Prittwitz, sent for the best staff officer on the Western Front, General Erich Ludendorff, who had lately distinguished himself in reducing the Belgian fortress complex, and selected from the retired list a new commanding officer who had

19   General Paul von Hindenburg and General Erich Ludendorff

been 'known for his imperturbability'. General Paul von Hindenburg was sixty-seven years old. The uniform which he wore was the old blue of Prussia, now universally superseded by field grey. He had no details of his command, deployment, or order of battle. Few of the officers were known to him, and Ludendorff he met for the first time that night on the express from Hanover. But the efficiency of the German military machine was such, and the training of those who operated it so thorough, that within hours of the arrival at Bartenstein of the new team the plans for VIII Army's next battle were being put into operation.

Hoffmann, together with Major-General Kersten (the Director of Railways *Ost*), had already devised the new schedule, which entailed switching all three corps that had fought at Gumbinnen some 70 miles south-west and placing them in position where they could envelope the advancing Samsonov.

François, so far undefeated, was turned in the widest arc, to take position on the far right where he could strike from the south and west into Samsonov's rear. Mackensen side-stepped behind the cover of the Rominten forest, to a point where he could move either against Samsonov's right or, if the need arose, interpose himself between the 'Warsaw' army and Rennenkampf. Below, at the rate of twenty-two trains a day, was filling the centre and bringing reinforcement to the depleted Scholtz.

While the Germans redeployed Samsonov continued his forward lunge. Jilinsky's tone became more urgent, the appeals for haste came twice a day, after the battle of Gumbinnen when it seemed that the Germans might 'escape'. Accordingly, the Russians seldom halted. Men and horses went short of sleep and food for day after day, while their supplies got lost or diverted and their movement orders repeated, countermanded, muddled. The two corps on Samsonov's right held different ciphers, neither having the key to that used by the other. Samsonov solved the communication problem which this presented by issuing his orders *en clair* over the radio.

Aerial reconnaissance was not much practised, partly because most of the Russian aircraft were positioned opposite the Austrians, partly because those that remained had learned to avoid the front line where their own men fired extravagantly at everything which came out of the skies. Such help as might have come from this quarter was still further frustrated by the rule that reports should first be sent to Jilinsky who, as has been seen, had his own preconceived ideas on the course of the battle. Furthermore the range of the Russian scouts – about 70 miles – was no longer enough adequately to support Samsonov whose own supply problems left no room for arranging fuel at advanced landing grounds. Consequently such air activity as there was took place on Rennenkampf's front where the pilots could, indeed, report that the Germans were retreating.

At this stage it must still have seemed, from Baranovichi where General Staff HQ were situated, that a tremendous Russian victory was in the making. It is all the more surprising then, to learn from the French ambassador's diary that ' . . . Jilinsky considers that an offensive in East Prussia is doomed to defeat', and that 'Janushkevich agrees, and is said to be protesting strongly against the offensive'. Then, suddenly the picture began to change. In the last forty-eight hours ground Intelligence began to identify a host of new, and fresh German units and the realisation dawned on Samsonov that the enemy had redeployed and were closing in on his flanks. In particular, he felt the danger on his extreme left, where François's corps was regrouping. Accordingly, Samsonov despatched one of his staff to HQ with a request to alter the axis of advance so that the Russian rear would not be so gravely threatened. From Jilinsky the message came back 'to see the enemy where he does not exist is cowardice. I will not allow General Samsonov to play the coward. I insist that he continue the offensive.'

THE TRAP CLOSES

The moment had come for Hindenburg to spring the trap. From the German side the risks still seemed enormous. In the centre they were outnumbered by more than two to one and facing some of the best troops in the Imperial Russian Army. It was feared that the centre might give way before the flanks could converge, that one of the flank attacks might fail or, worse, that the 'Vilna' army might speed its approach. 'Rennenkampf's formidable host hung like a threatening thunder-cloud to the north-east,' wrote Ludendorff in his memoirs, ' . . . he need only have closed with us and we should have been beaten.'

On 25th August, with Scholtz still under pressure and giving ground in the centre, Hindenburg gave orders to begin the encirclement. That evening the German intercept service caught two vital messages, one from Rennenkampf, which revealed his objective line for the next day and that he would be in no position to intervene in strength for at least three days after that; the second from Samsonov which revealed that he would

20   The Tsar and Duke Nicholas inspect élite regiments

continue to press his centre forward – into the noose. As Barbara Tuchman has so trenchantly observed, 'No such boon had ever been granted to a commander since a Greek traitor guided the Persians round the pass at Thermopylae.'

While the Germans strained every nerve to perfect their new dispositions in time Samsonov, forbidden to alter his own, vainly threshed the air with his right wing as he searched for the cavalry outriders of Rennenkampf's left. The Russian 6th Corps, ordered to stand fast on the afternoon of the 25th, was then instructed to break camp and move towards the centre 'with all speed' during the night. These orders were then countermanded on the morning of the 26th by which time the corps was already strung out in column of march. At mid-day the 6th Corps was under attack from Mackensen at its easterly end, while those of its divisions who had marched furthest west (in obedience to the orders of the night) now obediently returning and in a state of complete exhaustion, were caught by Below's advance guard across their route and cut to pieces.

In the centre, where the two crack commanders Martos and Kliouev were pressing hard against Scholtz, this disaster had an immediate effect. Kliouev had closed up to Scholtz's left after taking Allenstein, believing (in the context of the night orders) that 6th Corps would be covering his own left. In essence this meant that Samsonov's right flank had moved some 30 miles sideways – and was perilously exposed. The entire wing that comprised 6th Corps had been amputated and all prospect of tactical contact with Rennenkampf had gone with it.

On the morning of 27th August a tremendous bombardment to the west presaged the start of François's attack. By the afternoon the half-starved and exhausted Russian foot had broken, and Martos and

21 & 22   German postcards illustrate the battle of extermination at Tannenberg

Kliouev were stranded in the centre, cut off in the swamp and forest territory south of Tannenberg, in the old training grounds of the Prussian army which every regular officer knew by heart.

For three days a terrible battle of extermination was fought out in these dark woodlands:

> Some of the horrors of it are so ghastly that an eye witness, an officer, who has just returned from there says it will live in his dreams until his dying day.
>
> The sight of thousands of Russians driven into two huge lakes or swamps to drown was ghastly, and the shrieks and cries of the dying men and horses he will never forget. So fearful was the sight of these thousands of men with their guns, horses, and ammunition struggling in the water, that, to shorten their agony, they turned the machine-guns on them. But even in spite of that there was movement seen among them for a week after. And the mowing down of the cavalry brigade at the same time, 500 mounted men on white horses, all killed and packed so closely that they remained standing. The officer said that this sight was the ghastliest of the whole war.

The battle of Tannenberg extinguished prematurely, and finally, the Russian threat to Germany in direct encounter. But indirectly – by their victories over the Habsburg armies in the south – the Russian armies could still exert strategic pressure on her. It was also a hideous blow at the potency of the Russian military machine which, in the northern theatre, saw the cream of its officer corps and its accumulated supplies skimmed off before the war was a month old. Yet for all that, the Tannenberg campaign had achieved its strategic purpose. By sticking – even at such frightful cost – to their role in the Allied plan (which meant, in effect, doing what the French told them), by forcing their mobilisation and committing themselves prematurely to battle, the Russians had alarmed the German High Command enough to induce that critical diversion of force from the West against which Schlieffen had so earnestly counselled.

In St Petersburg, people were stunned by the news of the débâcle. General A.A.Noikov recorded their reactions:

> In the early morning of 1st September, while on my way to the offices of our General Staff, I noticed an unusual animation along the Nevski Prospekt. I kept passing groups of people engrossed in very lively discussions. An especially large group was gathered before the bulletin boards of the *Novoye Vremya*, Russia's leading newspaper, at the corner of Sadovia Street. I was somewhat surprised, for I had never seen so many

people there. Certainly an event of exceptional importance must have occurred at the Front. People looked upset, and a voice choked with emotion said: 'What a disaster! Even generals have been killed! Why is the government deceiving us with news of victories?' To which another voice added: 'It's exactly the same mess that happened during the war with Japan!'

Those words filled me with great anxiety. I pushed my way through the crowd and there was the bad news, a telegram from our Commander-in-Chief, Grand Duke Nicholas Nicolayevich:

'Following the arrival of reinforcements from all parts of the Front, large German forces supported by a highly developed railroad network have launched a massive attack against two of our army corps. Extremely violent artillery fire caused heavy losses among our troops, which fought heroically. General Samsonov, Martos, Pestiche, and several staff officers were killed. Measures that will enable us to avenge this unhappy event have been taken. The commander-in-chief trusts, as ever, that God will grant us victory.'

I could hardly believe my eyes, yet, there it was written: a great defeat! How was that possible? . . .

The appalling news spread like wildfire throughout the city. By noontime, thousands of relatives and friends of officers belonging to Samsonov's ill-fated army were gathered around General HQ. All were eager to obtain details on the disaster and to learn the fate of their beloved ones . . . .

The wildest rumours began to circulate. Some ladies, their eyes full of tears, gave harrowing descriptions, received God knows where, of the terrible catastrophe. According to them, the number of killed amounted to 100,000, and horrible scenes had taken place in the forests of East Prussia. No one, they said, had escaped the German trap . . . .

3

The Defeat of Count Conrad

THE ANNIHILATION of Samsonov's army – the very head of the lance which the Tsar had thrust at Prussia – when seen against a background of administrative chaos, complete lack of the most rudimentary security precautions, and a widespread defeatism both at Court and among broad sections of the politically articulate, made the prospect of Russia playing any further effective part in the war during 1914 seem slight. Yet, by the end of the year, the Grand Duke Nicholas had deployed an additional three armies in their entirety, had smashed the Austrians beyond recovery, and had fought the Germans to a standstill in Poland.

Partly it is true that the very inefficiencies of the Russian scene, the wasteful duplication of function and authority, kept the machine going under conditions that would have stopped one more dependent on a centralised system. Also the tremendous mobilisation scheme now, in the late autumn of 1914, coming to maturity gave the Russian armies that massive numerical superiority which the Central powers had always dreaded, and which was compounded by their own distraction with critical battles in other theatres – Austria in Serbia, the Germans at 'First Ypres'. It is also the case that in the south and – in numerical terms – over the major part of the Front, the Russians were opposed by a regime almost as inefficient as their own and without even the stoic courage and tenacity which sustained the *moujhik* soldiers even through the contrived disasters of their own leaders' incompetence.

The failings of the Austrian army were soon apparent, in the opening battles in Galicia. Nominally under the command of the Archduke Friedrich, their actual direction was in the hands of the Chief-of-Staff, Count Conrad von Hötzendorf. Conrad was in his sixties, short of stature, with a leathery wrinkled face and a white moustache longer and better-groomed than, for example, that of Earl Haig. In the course of some forty years of military service he had absorbed, it must be assumed, some rudiments of strategic theory. However, his serene aristocratic detachment and overt contempt for the peasant rank and file made him

23   The Tsar, holding an icon, blesses his troops

24   Count Conrad von Hotzendorf, the Austrian Chief-of-Staff

less than competent to direct an army whose numbers, at the end of mobilisation, approached 2,000,000. Conrad had witnessed from his childhood the steady erosion of the Habsburg Empire, the waxing of the 'nationalities', and the changing social orders which their humble bourgeois leaders personified. He had a simple solution – war – and the instrument lay in his own hand. As, according to the precepts of 18th-century surgery, the more severe the blood-letting the greater the likelihood of a cure.

A CUMBERSOME AND ARCHAIC ARMY

Unfortunately, the Habsburg army, though containing some excellent human material, suffered from a cumbersome and archaic organisation, and unimaginative and out-of-date training programmes. All promotion was within the prerogative of His Majesty the Emperor of Austria and Apostolic King of Hungary – as Franz Josef was entitled. Thus the centre of influence and intrigue remained where it had been for centuries – at the Palace – in an atmosphere hardly conducive to experiment or innovation.

The fragmentation of the various commands was an echo of feudal times when the great margraves would rally their private armies to the Emperor's standard; but now it was ministerial departments, instead of landowners, who maintained their separate jealousies. There was the Common Army (composed of professionals and conscripts together), the Austrian *Landwehr*, the Hungarian *Landwehr*, the *Landsturm*, and the Austrian, the Hungarian, and the Bosno-Herzegovinian *Gendarmeries*. Clothing and equipment for officers came from one corps of quartermasters, that for men from another department. Food was separate from animal fodder; field and mountain artillery was separate – having different ranks of seniority, and rates of pay – from fortress artillery.

Discipline was harsh. NCOs, for example, were not allowed to marry without permission from their commanding officer. Spies and *agents provocateurs* were scattered throughout the regiments made up of 'dissident' nationalities – whose officers were, almost without exception, Austrian or Hungarian. Equipment varied greatly from one regiment to another, although average fire-power was about equivalent to the Russian. Only in one arm did the Austrians have a clear superiority, and this was the massive howitzers from the Skoda works, better even than the best from Krupp, and used by the Germans in the siege train with which they had demolished the Belgian fortresses.

The original Austrian plan, Plan B, had envisaged immediate hostilities only with Serbia (using three armies), while a holding deployment would be maintained against Russia (with a further three armies). However, the Germans, having denuded Silesia and their whole front opposite the Polish salient, were desperate that their ally should press north-east against the Russian flank in Volnia so as to prevent the Polish salient from being used as a spring-board for an immediate invasion of the German centre.

A LAST-MINUTE CHANGE

At the last moment the Austrians switched to Plan R and Conrad threw the whole of his eastern strength across the frontier, into the Russian guns, without waiting for the III Army, pulled back from Serbia, to arrive on

25   Austro–Hungarian troops on their way to the front

26   Russian artillery take up position

the scene. Under Plan R (hostilities against Russia) only two armies were left facing Serbia, the V and VI. The III, which was allocated a major offensive share against Serbia in Plan B (Balkans) was to be deployed in the Galician plain with the I, II, and IV.

This in itself was perilous enough. The diverging axes of advance which the Austrian armies followed ensured first repulse, then disaster. In the summer of 1914, the main Austrian strength was in I Army, under General Dankl. Conrad had ordered Dankl to advance due north, with the intention of cutting the main Kiev-Warsaw railway between Lublin and Chełm. IV Army (General Auffenberg) was to advance north-east; III Army (General Brudermann) due east, in the direction of Rovno. Thus the Austrians, already outnumbered, were fanning out in a deployment that daily increased their frontage and diluted their strength.

For several days Dankl's men tramped northwards, singing their marching songs, running up the Habsburg flag in the captured townships. At night the regiments bivouacked, tents in rows, everything neatly furled as on manoeuvres, while the orderlies laid out the plate and linen in the officers' mess. Provisions were abundant; but in the heat; the pace of the advance, the sparsity of the opposition, the march of the Austrian I Army had ominous similarities with that of Samsonov's doomed battalions in East Prussia. On their right, the distance from Auffenberg, attacking Lutsk, widened daily; with Brudermann and the III Army soon held up before the fortress of Dubno, there was no proper liaison at all.

General Ivanov, the Russian commander of the South-West Front, at first watched the Austrian deployment with some perplexity. He had expected the enemy mass to advance east from Lemberg and had disposed his own armies with the highly unimaginative plan of meeting them head-on and fighting them to a standstill. The reports coming in showed that Brudermann was being blocked with little difficulty, but the cavalry of the weak Russian 4th Army (screening Dankl) told of a very large force now some 50 miles deep into Poland. Gradually, like some prehistoric monster responding to pain in a remote part of the body, Ivanov made his adjustments. Individual, more dashing, Russian army commanders did not share Ivanov's ingrained pessimism. Brusilov (who was to succeed him in 1916) rapidly worked his way round the enemy southern flank, and crossed the River Sereth below Tarnopol. General Nicholas Ruzsky, with the Russian 3rd Army, soon found the gap between Brudermann and Auffenberg and began to feel his way round the latter's right flank.

Most of the Austrian heavy artillery, the only arm with which they could match their adversary, was with Dankl, and owing to the speed of his advance, was not even in action there but spread out over the plains between Lublin and the River San. The unfortunate Brudermann, outgunned and outnumbered, with Brusilov behind his right flank and Ruzsky's wedge between him and Auffenberg's IV Army, began to fall back. During the first week in September 1914 Brudermann made two withdrawals, still more or less in good order though now completely isolated, and with Brusilov's cavalry roaming deep in his rear. It was 40 miles to the north-west, between Lutsk and the headwaters of the Bug, that the issue was decided. Here Auffenberg found himself in a pincer, between Ruzsky and a new Russian army, the 5th, under General Plehve. Attempting to stand and fight in this rolling, featureless country, without axial railway lines to bring supplies or relief, the Austrian army fast began to disintegrate. With Brudermann penned in and Auffenberg crumbling, no semblance of a 'front' remained. Dankl, still with the strongest – and as yet virtually untried – contingent, was completely unsupported, a gap over 50 miles across yawning on his right flank.

Count Conrad refused to accept the situation. Whether from ignorance (he still clung to the assumption that Ivanov's *masse de manoeuvre* was in the Lublin-Chełm area) or optimism (that the Russian advance in the south would peter out) or prestige (he believed himself to be within an ace of cutting the Kiev-Warsaw railway and bringing strategic relief to the Germans), Conrad continued to urge Dankl forward, the other two to 'stand fast'. On 8th September Plehve, having smashed Auffenberg's left, turned due west and placed himself directly behind Dankl. Two days of murderous fighting brought no relief to the Austrian I Army whose rail line was now severed, and on 11th September Conrad gave formal recognition to a situation already acted upon by his scattered and desperate corps commanders, and ordered a general retreat.

On 10th September the autumn rains had begun, still further worsening Dankl's plight, for, with Plehve across his communications, I Army's only course was a sideways shuffle into the river triangle between the San and the Vistula. Far to the south, Brusilov had forced the twin rivers of the Lipa, captured Halicz, and passed his cavalry divisions below Lemberg.

By 14th September it was plain, even to Conrad, that his command had simply disintegrated. Panic flight, mass desertion, and ruinous loss of heavy equipment left him with certain minimal solutions, namely the garrisoning of the great Przemyśl fortress which might, hopefully, bar Ivanov's access to the Dukla Pass and Hungary proper; second, the

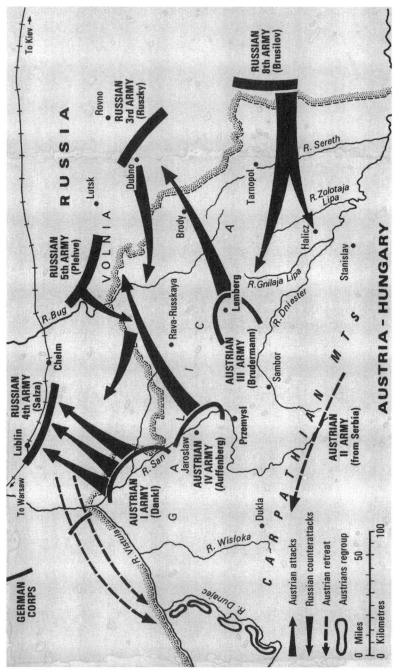

Conrad's road to disaster

possibility of rebuilding the remnants of Dankl's army along the line of the River Dunajec where, with the II Army now arriving from Serbia, they might defend Kraków on a shortened frontage. On this day a painful telephone conversation took place between Ludendorff and the Austro-Hungarian Supreme HQ at Neu-Sandec. In his memoirs Ludendorff records that Conrad's voice was 'calm and matter-of-fact', that his phrases were 'cautious'. On his own attitude he is less specific, but it is hard to believe that he made no protest on being told that the new line of resistance was to be not the San, nor the Wisłok, but the Dunajec – a retreat of some 140 miles!

The effect of Conrad's defeat, in strategic terms, was that the whole

27   General von Rennenkampf

German southern flank in Poland and Silesia was wide open, their position far more serious than if Conrad had never moved at all, and had, after all, stuck to Plan B. Fortunately however, while the Austrian army had been collapsing, the victors of Tannenberg had turned on Rennenkampf and driven him from East Prussia following the Battle of the Masurian Lakes.

Rennenkampf had, at least, avoided Conrad's mistake of waiting too long before issuing the order to retreat. Behind a valiant rearguard which had frustrated the German envelopment the Russians had galloped eastward, back across their own frontiers. Rennenkampf moved his HQ three times in one day, finally issuing his orders from a moving Delaunay-Belleville staff car. The methodical Germans, busy counting booty and rounding up stragglers in the forests, could not keep up, and the combatants became separated. On 14th September, the same day that Conrad had confessed defeat in the south to Ludendorff, Rennenkampf telegraphed to the Grand Duke that 'All corps have now broken off the battle'.

THE INDECISIVE BLOODLETTING

The war was now six weeks old. Actual fighting had occupied little more than a month. Yet combined casualties already approached 750,000. The massed battalions of the three great European empires had marched and countermarched over immense tracts of territory, swaying and bleeding in a sequence of desperate, extravagant, but, with the exception of Moltke's (unnecessary) diversion of strength from the West before Tannenberg, strategically indecisive encounters. While the fighting in the West hardened, the soldiers burrowed deep, and the battlefield showed only the curling earth breastworks of freshly-dug trench lines, a place where no man could stand upright without drawing forth the hollow stutter of machine-gun fire, in the East it was still a different era.

In those first weeks the mobilisation and reinforcement rate surpassed – numerically though not in quality – the frightful casualties even of Tannenberg and Galicia. The generals could draw comfort that, in almost every case the forces under command were greater than those which they had originally committed to battle. And so each side now set itself to stage still more ambitious and extravagant offensives. If the war was to be ended by Christmas, time was running short.

The soldiers still wore their peacetime uniform, the cavalry helmets gleamed and the brass-inlaid gun carriages caught the light. They, and

28   Austrian prisoners taken in the Russian counterattack

their commanders – archdukes, grand dukes, Baltic barons, scions of the landed aristocracy – were blind to the truth. For as Lenin perceived, in fighting each other to the death they were putting the entire social order (which both had in common) in jeopardy.

This truth is well illustrated by an extract from the diary of Maurice Paléologue, the French ambassador in St Petersburg:

> One of my informers, B, who has personal contacts in radical circles, tells me that they are eagerly discussing a strange thesis advanced by the anarchist Lenin, who is a refugee in Switzerland.
>
> A convinced disciple of Karl Marx, and the leader of the Maximalist Social-Democrats, Lenin proclaims that Russia's military defeat must be the prelude to the Russian revolution and the very condition of its success. Consequently, he is urging the Russian proletariat to facilitate the victory of the Germans by all possible means.
>
> 'But,' I replied, 'how can the victory of Germany, that is of German militarism, ever benefit the Russian revolution? In breaking free from the yoke of Tsarism, Russia would merely fall into the bondage of Prussian absolutism!'
>
> I am not qualified to demonstrate Lenin's thesis. For a long time he has

stressed that the Russian revolution must be the model of all social revolutions, that it must therefore destroy the idea of fatherland in the minds of the Russian people, and that all other peoples will surely follow the example of Russia.

'Isn't Lenin an *agent provocateur* paid by Germany?'

'No! He is not a corruptible man. He is an exalted and fanatic fellow, but he also has a conscience. He is respected by all.'

'That makes him all the more dangerous.'

Thus both extremes of the Russian society, the intransigent supporters of orthodox Tsarism as well as the rabid advocates of complete anarchism, have one great wish in common: the victory of Germany!'

It was true also that these men were floundering in an element of which they had neither experience nor comprehension. The very scale of these enormous – super-Napoleonic – battles was beyond their powers. It was beyond, too, the simple techniques of communication – radios, telephones, the mechanical devices that gave speed and flexibility. These things were simply not developed to a pitch where, except in a small and familiar area such as the Tannenberg battlefield, the great masses could be intelligently used.

It soon became apparent, though, even to the victors of the day, that things were not as they should be. And so the clash of personalities, of private intrigue and ambition dormant at the outset began, as will be seen in the following chapter, to compound the difficulties of strategic planning.

29   Austrian prisoners waiting to be evacuated

4

German Victories in Poland

FOLLOWING the victory at Tannenberg, Ludendorff and Hoffmann began to conceive the plan for a major German strategic envelopment of the entire Russian strength in Poland. This project, which was repeatedly discussed over the next twelve months, depended on a concentrated attack east-south-east out of the Masurian Lakes, wheeling down between Vilna and Grodno to cut the main Moscow railway *behind* Brest-Litovsk. Highly ambitious as this plan was, it had small chance of success unless the Germans received substantial reinforcement from the West, or the Russians became more seriously depleted in conventional operations in the centre. It depended, too, on at least a semblance of support from the Austrian army in the south.

Having spoken to Conrad on the telephone on 14th September Ludendorff realised at once that there could be no prospect of a major offensive in the north; for the Austrians were in no position to co-operate, and were plainly going to have to draw on German strength in order to be able to survive at all. That additional German strength should be drawn eastward into their own theatre was welcome to Ludendorff and Hindenburg who now believed, and intended, that the war should be decided there, and by them. What was important was to ensure that this strength was an accretion rather than a rival to their own forces (as would be the case if it were placed under Conrad, or some fresh nominee of Supreme HQ General Staff).

Ludendorff had also spoken to Moltke on the evening of 14th September, and in the course of a long conversation marred by frequent interruptions (the telephone line stretched from Insterburg to Belgium) had persuaded him that it would be 'inadvisable' to detach two corps from VIII Army to form a new army in the south, and that East Prussia could now be safely garrisoned by fortress troops and the whole of VIII Army – with, of course, its commander and staff – should be moved down onto the Austrian flank.

The following day, though, Moltke was relieved, and his successor,

30   German troops man a trench line in East Prussia during the autumn of 1914. Shallow, linear trenches such as this were soon shown up as death traps

31   A German soldier on border patrol between East Prussia and Russian Poland

General Erich von Falkenhayn, was to prove of very different calibre. He was 'tall and slim, with a particularly youthful face, in which were a pair of very sharp and clever but sarcastic eyes, with the striking contrast of a very grey, but very thick, head of hair'. Falkenhayn was a cynic, and a pessimist. He had come from the *Bendlerstrasse* – was, indeed, Minister for War – and took a gloomy view of prospects. The war would be a long one, Falkenhayn believed, and it was his duty to conserve the resources of the fatherland, not to lavish them on his subordinates – ' . . . the lies that these army commanders combine in telling are quite incredible', was his comment after his first visit to the Front. It is possible that Falkenhayn, who had seen the German offensive at the Marne crumble at Moltke's nervous touch ('Schlieffen's notes do not help any further, and so Moltke's wits come to an end!') then tried himself to retrieve it at the First Battle of Ypres and failed, already believed that the war could not be won. Certainly he never believed that it could be won in the East, and the whole course of German operations in this theatre in 1915 is coloured by the contest of wills between Falkenhayn, who wanted a holding operation, and Ludendorff, who sought a decisive solution.

In late September the Russian mobilisation was at full tide. The Grand Duke Nicholas called an army commanders' conference at Kholm on 22nd September, and gave his orders for a new offensive, to be opened in three weeks' time and which was intended to carry the Russian armies to the Oder. Morale in the army was at its peak; the huge tracts of conquered Austrian territory and the mass of booty, the evidence on every side of accumulating strength, had combined to erase the uncomfortable memory of Tannenberg, which was depicted as a 'local' affair, with no significant loss of ground and where, indeed, Rennenkampf was already feeling his way back across the enemy frontier. The Tsar, greatly heartened after the sweeping Russian victories against Austria-Hungary, had sent for the French ambassador and spent an enjoyable afternoon in December 1914 discussing the changes which he would insist upon in the new Europe: 'The Tsar lit his cigarette, offered me a light, and went straight to the heart of the subject:

> 'Great things have happened in the three months since I saw you last. The splendid French army and my dear army have already given such proofs of valour that victory can't fail us now. Don't think I am under any illusion as to the trials and sacrifices the war still has in store for us; but so far we

have a right, and even a duty, to consult together what we should have to do if Austria or Germany sue for peace.

We must *dictate* the peace. I am determined to continue the war until the Central powers are destroyed. I regard it as essential that the terms of peace should be discussed by us three – France, England, and Russia – and by us three alone. No congress or mediation for me! . . .

What we must keep before us as our first objective is the destruction of German militarism, the end of the nightmare from which Germany has made us suffer for the last forty years. We must make it impossible for the German people even to think of revenge. If we let ourselves be swayed by sentiment there will be a fresh war within a very short time.'

He drew his chair close to mine, spread a map of Europe on the table between us, lit another cigarette, and continued in an even more intimate and familiar tone:

'This is more or less my view of the results Russia is entitled to expect from the war. In East Prussia Germany must accept a rectification [sic] of the frontier. My General Staff would like this rectification extended to the mouth of the Vistula. That seems to me excessive; I'll look into the questions. Poznania and possibly a portion of Silesia will be indispensable to the reconstitution of Poland. Galicia and the western half of the Bukovina will enable Russia to obtain her natural frontiers, the Carpathians. In Asia Minor I shall have to consider the question of the Armenians, of course; I certainly could not let them return to the Turkish yoke. Lastly, I shall be compelled to secure my Empire a free passage through the Straits . . .

There are two conclusions to which I am always being brought back; first that the Turks must be expelled from Europe; secondly, that Constantinople must in the future be neutral, with an international regime . . .'

Then he spread out a map of the Balkans and indicated broadly his view of the territorial changes we should desire. [These were followed by a general résumé of territorial distribution in the West – the Kiel Canal to Denmark, Aachen to Belgium etc. etc., which foreshadowed the 1944 Morgenthau Plan coupled with the most rapacious of the Russian demands at Yalta.]

'Our work cannot be justified before God and history unless it is inspired by a great moral idea and the determination to secure the peace of the world for a very long time to come . . .'

The Tsar's attitude may be read in conjunction with the note on the European alliance system in the preface to this book and as an illustration of the inherent perils in upsetting any political balance by armed conflict.

A HEAD-ON COLLISION

For the new offensive no ambitious timing or deployment was called for. The Grand Duke's plan was for a straightforward march, due west, into a head-on collision with the defenders, who would be trampled to death. The victors of Galicia, powerfully reinforced, were lined up in a phalanx over 1,250,000 strong. In the south, Brusilov and Ruzsky besieged Przemyśl on 16th September and faced the remnants of Conrad's Austrian army across the River Dunajec. A complete new Russian army, the 9th, stood on their right at the confluence of the San; then Salza's 4th Army at Ivangorod; then Plehve below Warsaw and, on the extreme right, a 'reconstituted' 2nd Army. In terms of quality and equipment these armies represented the peak of Russian strength in the First World War. But they were living on capital. Magazines were full, and inventories complete, but the pipeline was dry. Muddle and corruption had compounded industrial inefficiency to a state where the supply and maintenance of armies this size was simply beyond its capacity.

While the Grand Duke hastily assembled his provisions for this new forward lunge the Germans, with their faster communications, slid down across his line of advance to attack from the right. Falkenhayn, having created the new IX Army, to look after the southern sector, transferred to it the senior command structure of VIII Army (although many of the best corps and divisional commanders remained in the north). Ludendorff proposed to throw IX Army against the Grand Duke's flank on the Vistula, catching the Russians off-balance before their own forward movement could get under way. However, as IX Army possessed only eighteen divisions against a Russian strength of at least sixty, it was essential that the Austrians should also move forward in the south in order to give some protection to the German flank.

Naturally, Conrad did nothing, and once IX Army had reached the Vistula between Warsaw and Ivangorod they ran into heavy fighting which soon drew in all local reserves. Within days Plehve, virtually unopposed on his own front, started to wheel southward, threatening to encircle the whole of IX Army, or force it back against the guns of the fresh troops from the Caucasus on the left bank of the Vistula. Hoffmann's diary records ' . . . the hardest time of the campaign in my experience: the strain goes on day and night – endless panics and alarms. . . . Ludendorff and I stand by and support each other, and the Chief [Hindenburg] just says, "God be with us. I can do no more." '

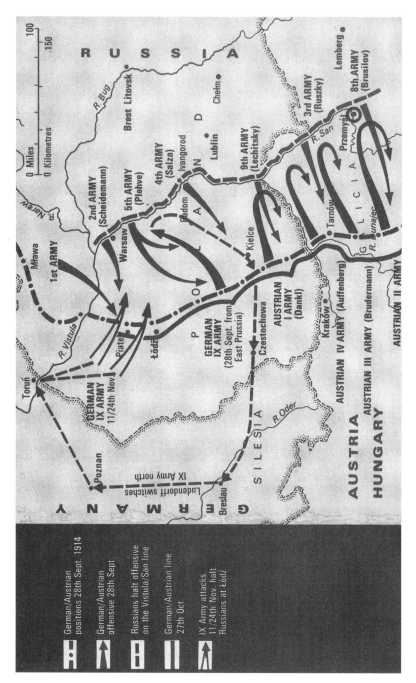

The German and Russian offensives of autumn and winter, 1914

32   Russian artillery moving forward

Conrad refused an appeal from Ludendorff, who then got Hindenburg
to ask the Kaiser to make a personal request to the Emperor Franz Josef.
The old man, however, 'declined to interfere in the military conduct of
the war'. A similar aloofness was shown by Falkenhayn who ignored
appeals for the old VIII Army as reinforcement, sending the XV Reserve
Corps to East Prussia instead. 'Ludendorff has become frightfully
nervous,' wrote Hoffmann, ' . . . if we had been given only two or three
more corps here I could have guaranteed a decision. . . .'

As pressure on the left wing mounted, the Austrians, at last goaded into
action, had got into difficulties immediately and Conrad had begun a
withdrawal. Inter-Allied harmony was not improved by a wireless
intercept of an order to the Austrian I Army to retreat at once, ' . . . but
the German Guard Reserve Corps [on its left] is not to be informed of
this until 6 o'clock this evening'.

On 27th October, after three weeks of confused and bloody fighting,
the Germans withdrew. Again making full use of their undamaged railway
system, IX Army completely eluded its pursuers, though ceding a wide
belt of territory between the Vistula and Łódź. The Russians, although
somewhat disorganised and having expended copious quantities of their

precious ammunition, were still menacing. Ludendorff calculated that they would be coming forward against the end of November, and this time their momentum would carry them into Germany itself. He saw also that there was still one sector where they were vulnerable. Plehve's wheel to the south had opened a wide gap between his 5th Army and the new 2nd Army (now commanded by Scheidemann). If the Germans could travel fast enough around the perimeter of the Russian salient they could strike at this exposed sector before their enemies' redeployment was complete.

Within ten days IX Army had completed its circular tour, back from Kielce to Czestochowa and then round on the parallel German military system through Kempen and Poznan to Toruń. Without giving his men any rest, Ludendorff at once forced the new attack – a wedge driven between the Russian 1st and 2nd Armies, down the west bank of the Vistula, to cut the railway between Lódz and Warsaw. Again, as in the September battles, the Germans were heavily outnumbered and again the

33   Russian artillery bombard Przemyśl during the siege

34 Russian artillery traverse a river

slow but tenacious enemy reaction gradually squeezed their spearhead into a perilous situation. The iron discipline and training of the Germans – particularly Scheffer's XXV Corps – did much to compensate for the fact that they were outnumbered by four to one, but once battle was joined their superior mobility was no longer such an advantage. At the end of November both sides were glad to break off the action and retire to their winter lines. But if on the map the results of Łódź and the Vistula look inconclusive, strategically they added up to a Russian defeat. The Grand Duke's winter offensive had never got under way and his reserves – of material if not of men – had been seriously depleted.

Ludendorff now returned to his theme of a great outflanking stroke from the north and devoted himself, throughout the opening months of 1915, to lobbying – directly at HQ through Hindenburg, by approaches to the Kaiser – for a massive reinforcement of *Oberost (Oberbefehlshaber der deutschen Streitkräfte im Osten)* – the new command which had recently been promulgated, and included both VIII and IX Armies. Falkenhayn, however, remained undecided. When Ludendorff detached a number of divisions from *Oberost* to support Conrad (a technical device which he hoped would lead to a supreme command of both German *and* Austrian forces in the East), Falkenhayn promptly formed them into an independent new army and ordered Ludendorff himself to report to it as

*Kowno.
An der Notbrücke
über den Njemen.*

35   German troops making their way across a pontoon bridge

chief-of-staff! Hindenburg was called in to write a personal appeal to the Kaiser for the return of his indispensable aide. A meeting took place at Breslau on 11th January, at which Falkenhayn's suave courtesy made a disagreeable impression ' . . . it was all unsatisfactory and pointless, a contest of opinions settled beforehand', wrote Ludendorff in his diary. Not content with securing his own return to Hindenburg's side, Ludendorff now forced his chief to request the Kaiser that Falkenhayn be dismissed. Somewhat surprised (it may be thought) the Kaiser compromised by arranging that Falkenhayn would resign as Minister of War, though remain as Chief of the General Staff.

Meanwhile the Grand Duke Nicholas had decided to make a further – and final – major offensive. This time the main weight would fall on the Austrians, with diversionary blows in Poland and East Prussia to tie down possible German reinforcement. Throughout the early spring the Russians gradually improved their position, though serious shortages crippled many units.

THE LONG, TERRIBLE SUMMER

By late spring 1915, the Russians were holding a huge salient which stretched deep into Poland and Austria-Hungary. The elimination of this became the major strategic objective of the German High Command

The Front Line, May to September 1915

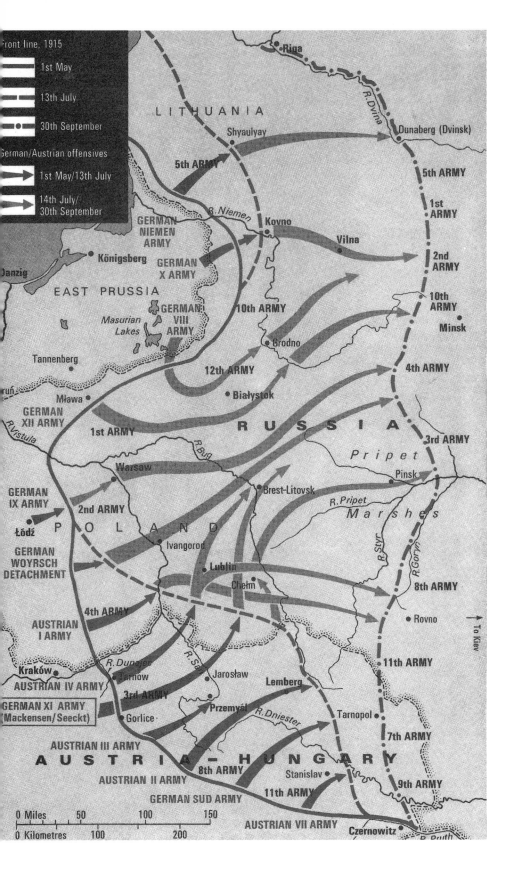

Front line, 1915

1st May

13th July

30th September

German/Austrian offensives

1st May/13th July

14th July/
30th September

LITHUANIA

Riga

R. Dvina

R. Niemen

Shyaulyay

Dunaberg (Dvinsk)

5th ARMY

5th ARMY

GERMAN
NIEMEN
ARMY

Königsberg

Kovno

Vilna

1st
ARMY

Danzig

GERMAN X ARMY

2nd
ARMY

EAST PRUSSIA

GERMAN
VIII
ARMY

10th ARMY

10th
ARMY

Masurian
Lakes

Grodno

Minsk

Tannenberg

12th ARMY

4th ARMY

Mława

Białystok

3rd ARMY

GERMAN
XII ARMY

1st ARMY

R U S S I A

R. Vistula

R. Bug

Pripet

Toruń

Warsaw

Brest-Litovsk

Pinsk

GERMAN
IX ARMY

2nd ARMY

P O L A N D

R. Pripet

Marshes

Łódź

Ivangorod

8th ARMY

GERMAN
WOYRSCH
DETACHMENT

Lublin

Chełm

R. Styr

R. Goryn

4th ARMY

AUSTRIAN
I ARMY

Rovno

R. Dunajec

R. San

11th ARMY

Kraków

Tarnów

Jarosław

Lemberg

AUSTRIAN IV ARMY

3rd ARMY

Przemyśl

R. Dniester

Tarnopol

7th ARMY

GERMAN XI ARMY
(Mackensen/Seeckt)

Gorlice

To Kiev

AUSTRIA – HUNGARY

AUSTRIAN III ARMY

8th ARMY

Stanislav

9th ARMY

AUSTRIAN II ARMY

GERMAN SUD ARMY

11th ARMY

0 Miles 50 100 150

0 Kilometres 100 200

AUSTRIAN VII ARMY

Czernowitz

R. Pruth

36   The German General Mackensen

37   German and Austrian troops entering the fallen city of Przemyśl

since from it the Russians could threaten any overland route to Turkey. Secretly, therefore, a new XI Army was created under Mackensen to smash into the south of the Russian salient between Tarnow and Gorlice where it was weakest. The German assault was brilliantly successful. By the middle of July the Russians had been thrown back from almost all Austro-Hungarian territory and they continued to be herded eastwards until their pursuers had to halt for lack of reinforcements. The horrors of the long retreat and the serious deficiencies in equipment which it highlighted, played a serious part in destroying morale both at the front and at home. On 21st March they finally forced the surrender of Przemyśl, taking 120,000 prisoners, and thus clearing the approaches to the Carpathians.

The fall of Przemyśl occurred in the same week as the naval attempt (not the landing) by the British to force the Dardanelles. Together the two seem to have persuaded Falkenhayn, who was now aiming for a negotiated stalemate, that the first condition of any talks must be the elimination of Serbia and the establishment of a secure overland route to Turkey. It had become essential that Russian troops be thrown out of Austrian territory – what might happen in north Poland and Masuria was strategically irrelevant. At the end of April, therefore, the new XI Army was created, and charged with the express purpose of shattering the Grand Duke's southern wing. XI Army was four corps strong and placed under the command of Mackensen and Seeckt. Its divorcement from *Oberost* was emphasised by the restriction that, although under the nominal command of Conrad, it was agreed that no orders would be issued to it without Falkenhayn's approval.

As usual, poor Russian Intelligence had failed to reveal the appearance of German troops on a front which they believed to be held by Austrians. Between Gorlice and Tarnow there were only six Russian divisions, without rear defence lines and little artillery. Against this Falkenhayn had pitted the whole of Mackensen's army, 1,500 guns, and seven Austrian divisions. The attack opened on 2nd May and surprise was complete. Mackensen's army advanced at the rate of 10 miles per day, reaching the River San on 14th May. From the Carpathian foothills Brusilov's 8th Army struggled northward, arriving just in time to hold the river line for a few days while stragglers poured across and the Grand Duke's armies in the centre pulled back their flank, now for the fourth time, over to the east bank of the Vistula.

Brusilov had virtually no artillery with which to counter the massed

German batteries, and a fresh assault in June levered his army away from the San, carrying Mackensen on to Lemberg and the old lines of September 1914. To the north the Grand Duke, who had been delaying his own offensive while waiting for new equipment, folded back and extended his flank to match each new advance by the enemy. By midsummer the great Polish salient had returned to its original shape – though now with Germans around the whole perimeter instead of only in the north. Still more ominous was the material reduction in the Russian fighting capacity.

The Chief-of-Staff reported to the French ambassador that ' . . . we are not producing more than 24,000 shells a day. It's a pittance for so vast a front! But our shortage of rifles alarms me far more. Just think! In several infantry regiments that have taken part in the recent battles *at least one third of the men had no rifle.* These poor devils had to wait patiently under a shower of shrapnel until their comrades fell before their eyes and they could pick up their arms . . . .'

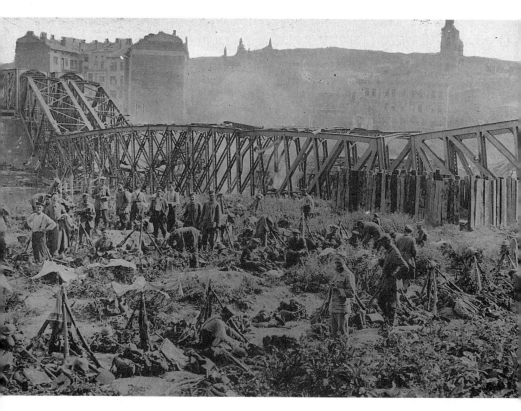

38   German troops examine the ruins of the bridge over the Vistula at Przemyśl

Salza, the commander of IV Army, which had defeated Dankl the previous autumn, wrote that ' . . . at the beginning of the war, when we had guns, ammunition, and rifles, we were the victors. When the supply of munitions and arms began to give out we still fought brilliantly. Today, with its artillery and infantry dumb, our army is drowning in its own blood!'

This was a time of universal shortage – of the 'Shells Scandal' and changes of government in the West – when even the French batteries were restricted to fifty rounds per day, and the English to five. But on this one thing the Western leaders were agreed – that Russia must not be allowed to drop out of the war. While their ill-starred 'diversionary' offensives butted at the German line in France, convoys of precious supplies crept along the north and south passages to Russian ports. After Turkey entered the war Russia had become, in Golovine's analogy, 'A barred house which could only be entered through the chimney'. Masses of material unloaded at Salonika lay on the quay for months, was then reloaded and consigned to Archangel, via Gibraltar, Biscay, the Irish Channel, Cape Wrath, and Spitzbergen. For the whole of the northern winter Archangel was iced up and the steamers used to dump their cargoes at Alexandrovsk and other small ports on the Murmansk coast where shortage of rolling stock and the bad repair of the railways often confined them for the duration of the war.

Overland the journey was still more wasteful. Material purchased by the joint Allied Commission in the United States was shipped to Vladivostok, and there stacked for entrainment. The rail route was 3,500 miles long, and each supply train required 120 engines. Often trains would break down in the middle of the steppe, the engines would unhitch and they would be left in remote sidings, or the cargo would simply be jettisoned by the side of the single-track line, where it would remain for years, pillaged by nomads and bandits.

If every gun, bullet, and great-coat which the Allies sent to Russia had been delivered, the Grand Duke's armies would still, in that terrible summer campaign of 1915, have been perilously under-equipped. Forced away from their depots and railheads, huge masses of Russian infantry stumbled about in the dusty heat of the Polish summer, without co-ordination or hope of recovery. Mackensen had taken over 400,000 prisoners in the first stage of his offensive. Now he was turned about and directed north-east towards Lublin and the jugular artery of the Polish armies – the Warsaw-Minsk railway. Ludendorff, fretting impatiently meanwhile in East Prussia, was at last taken off the leash by Falkenhayn and attacked to the south, towards Roshan and Białystok.

A CHAIN-REACTION OF DEFEATISM

Once the army began to collapse, a chain-reaction of riot and defeatism began to spread through the Russian homeland. The French ambassador noted that ' . . . the disorders in Moscow have been particularly serious owing to one element to which the press descriptions have not alluded. The agitation assumed such a scale that it has become necessary to suppress it by force. On the Krasnaia Plochtad, the famous "Red Square" which has witnessed so many historical scenes, the mob insulted the Royal Family, demanded that the Empress should be incarcerated in a convent, the Emperor deposed, and the crown transferred to the Grand Duke Nicholas, Rasputin hung, etc. . . .'

At this stage the reaction of the 'general public' – if such a democratic-sounding term can be used of the mass of opinion in Tsarist Russia – was still essentially nationalist and patriotic. They identified, and with good reason, a prime source of weakness in the intrigue and personal corruption that pervaded the Empress's immediate circle. A few days after the riots Paléologue spoke to Suvorin, the editor of *Novoye Vremya*, who told him: 'I've lost all hope. We are doomed to disaster from now on.'

But the despair did not yet have that nihilist character which cleared the way for the Bolsheviks in 1917. The internal contest for influence and power was a hexagonal one, between the pro-German Baltic nobility, the Tsarina and Rasputin clique, the discontented *Tchinovniki*, the anti-German military, the Kerensky Socialists (at this stage stronger in the unions than the Bolsheviks), and the Tsar himself, pulled this way and that by competing factions, incapable of taking a decision, gloomily awaiting – as he was later to reveal – the moment of his abdication.

For three terrible months of high summer the Grand Duke fought his armies eastward, eluding – though often at a terrible cost – a succession of German encirclements. Then, in September, with the Front at last stabilised on a line from Riga to the River Pruth, he was relieved of his command and the Tsar himself took over.

This was, in terms of the internal politics of the Court, a victory for the Empress. It could not but have disastrous results on the conduct of the army in the field; it could have led, at best, only to a marked polarisation of control and policy under individual 'Front' and army

39 German troops resting after breakthrough in Poland

40 German postcard depicting victorious lancers entering Czenstochau in Russian Poland

commanders. Fortunately, though, there was to be no autumn campaign. Falkenhayn had been dismissed, and Ludendorff appointed in his place. Old Franz Josef died and his great-nephew the Archduke Karl ascended to the throne. Karl immediately took command of the army from his cousin Friedrich, and dismissed the fumbling (but pro-German) Conrad. Of the old cast only the cynical and brilliant Hoffmann remained, and he soon discovered to what extent his old chief's wider responsibilities had changed his attitude. When, in November, Hoffmann asked for reinforcements for a new offensive in the South toward Odessa, Ludendorff replied that although he ' . . . realised the strategic opportunity, regretfully no troops could be spared from the Western Front . . . .'

By the end of the year the Russian army was at every point back within its own frontiers, brutally mauled but having escaped mortal damage. Germany was looking West, and the real dangers which threatened St Petersburg came from within:

> I dined quite privately this evening with the most important metallurgist and financier in Russia, the multi-millionaire Putilov. He is one of the four industrialists who are members of the Munitions Council . . . . His first impressions were simply deplorable. It is not merely a technical problem, a question of labour and output, which has to be solved. The whole administrative system of Russia must be reformed from top to bottom.
>
> We discussed the future; he almost revelled in describing the fatal consequences of the imminent catastrophes and the silent work of decadence and dislocation which is undermining the Russian edifice:
>
> 'The days of Tsarism are numbered; it is lost, beyond hope. But Tsarism is the very framework of Russia and the sole bond of unity for the nation. Revolution is now inevitable; it is only waiting for a favourable opportunity. Such opportunity will come with some military defeat, a famine in the provinces, a strike in Petrograd, riot in Moscow, some scandal or tragedy in the Palace.' [In fact it needed all five of these, more or less simultaneously.]

5

The Brusilov Offensive

THROUGHOUT the (unusually mild) winter of 1915–16 the Russian army gradually recovered its strength. Fighting was sporadic, and light in character – arising usually more from accidents of timing than from tactical purpose. The men huddled over charcoal braziers in great rambling log and earth stockades, or sheltered in dugouts 20 feet below the hard-frozen surface. Miles and miles of 'front' neither heard a shot, nor even saw a soldier for months at a time, The 'Line' was an area, sometimes 20 or 25 miles wide, criss-crossed by marauding cavalry patrols searching for fodder and women.

Yet all through the winter the Russian industrial machine, now converted – though at ruinous cost in terms of efficiency and human welfare – on to a 'war footing', was grinding out supplies for the army. Communications were shorter, and more efficient. The great north-south railway from St Petersburg to Poltava, though too far behind the front

41   For the last time the Russians gathered all their strength : a supply convoy leaves for the Front

42   Russian field bakeries in the Carpathians

(as will be seen) to allow the rapid switching of large bodies of infantry, was ideally placed as a supply artery from which no fewer than seven east-west trunk lines could feed the army. Slowly, and amid great confusion, a mass of equipment – much of it unfamiliar – began to build up. Rifles, machine-guns, new artillery pieces designed by French ordnance experts, saddles, great-coats, even supplies of morphine and Lysol collected by Lady Georgina Buchanan's fund in London, found their way up to the line. The country's incredible powers of recuperation, which were, twenty-eight years later, once more to confound the Germans, now restored its army to, and beyond, the strength which it had enjoyed in the opening weeks of the war.

Nonetheless, the crippling casualties among both the officer corps and the trained NCOs of the regular cadres had left an indelible scar on the Russian army. Its old faults – clumsiness, sloth in exploitation and response – were emphasised, while dependence on its old standby of sheer numbers increased. At the inter-Allied conference at Chantilly, where the strategic objectives for 1916 were optimistically discussed, there was a tacit recognition that no major offensive role could be expected from the Russians in the first six months of 1916.

Ludendorff and the Staff of *Oberost* had, by contrast, devised an offensive plan of grandiose proportions. A wide left wheel to the Baltic which would cut off the Russians in Latvia and even, if all went well, open the road to St Petersburg itself. To their chagrin Falkenhayn, like the Western Allies, had decided that the war would be decided in France. At the end of January, about eight weeks after Joffre had laid down the Allies' planning for 1916, Falkenhayn summoned Ludendorff and Conrad to Lida. There he explained his intention to bleed the French army white

43   Russian troops wait at a river's edge

in *'Operation Gericht'* (place of execution) at Verdun. There was to be a generally defensive stance in the East. In particular, Falkenhayn refused Conrad's request to be allowed to stage an offensive against the Italians and warned him against any transfer of troops westward out of Galicia. (Conrad, as will be seen, ignored both these pieces of advice.)

If the belligerents had stuck to their projected programmes, the Eastern Front would have been quiet during most of the 1916 campaigning season. In fact, and in conformity with the pattern of previous years, the Western Allies soon got into trouble and had to send an urgent appeal to the Tsar for a diversion. The fall of Douaumont, the strongest fortress in the Verdun chain, precipitated a crisis of confidence in Paris and Maurice Paléologue, the ambassador in St Petersburg, had once again to request that sufficient pressure be exerted in the East to draw German soldiers away from France.

THE FALSE START

Chivalrous as ever, the Tsar responded. At the beginning of March two armies on Kuropatkin's front went over to the attack. The ground – between two lakes, Narotch and Vishinev – was particularly unsuitable as the spring thaw was about to begin, and within a few days the battlefield was a morass, cut by hundreds of icy rivulets from broken reservoirs and swollen rivers. Waist deep, the Russians continued to press forward, lacerated again and again from the cross-fire of a few well-sited machine-guns. On 17th March Kuropatkin's losses in dead were 9,700 – the German, 560. Yet Hoffmann recorded that, 'for three days the situation was critical'. Then, one by one, the Russian batteries fell silent while the German counterfire, plotted by Ludendorff's new discovery and protégé, the artillery expert Bruchmüller, battered the Russian rear. Within weeks Kuropatkin was back on his start line. Nothing had been achieved. There was no gain in territory, no strategic advantage. Only lives (and precious ammunition) had been expended.

Consequently it was in some gloom that the Front commanders – Kuropatkin (North-Western), Evert (West), and Brusilov (South-Western) – assembled at STAVKA (the Imperial Russian High Command) on 14th April 1916 for an audience with the Tsar. General opinion – held particularly strongly by staff and commanders facing German soldiers – was that the offensive was futile, and that resources were best conserved to meet an enemy attack expected during the summer.

General Alexey Brusilov, commander of the South-Western Front, was faced only by Austrians. He knew from Intelligence reports, from spies in the countryside and from prisoners, that a large part of the Habsburg army, and all the Czechs, were ready to desert. He knew also that some of the best divisions had been transferred to Italy. (Conrad, having given his word to Falkenhayn at Lida, had withdrawn no fewer than nine divisions from the armies in Poland!) Brusilov, to the dismay of his colleagues, and in some cases of his subordinates also, urged that the offensive should be prosecuted vigorously along the whole length of the battlefront.

Brusilov was a forceful, handsome, and relatively successful commander in his early fifties, whose intense patriotism and aristocratic connections recommended him to the Tsar. Skill and subtlety in argument were not, however, talents that he possessed. A more devious advocate, calculating that his case would inevitably be opposed in discussion, would have started by recommending one course, and then allowed his opponents'

44   General Alexey Brusilov, commander of the South-western Front

45   General Kuropatkin

arguments to steer him into accepting the 'compromise' which concealed his real intentions. Instead, Brusilov began by putting his case with great force and finished by accepting a second-best.

Brusilov argued that the great length of the battlefront could only be turned to the Russian advantage if their superior numbers were employed in simultaneous attacks. Otherwise the Germans could always use their superior speed, in manoeuvre and deployment, to protect any area in immediate danger.

It was indisputable that Conrad's army was the weakest point in the enemy line, and it was against him that the main attack should be delivered. But it was essential, Brusilov argued, that the Germans should be prevented from shoring up the Austrian position when it started to crumble, and this could only be achieved if they were tied down by simultaneous attacks in their own sectors.

The Tsar listened, but could not decide. Kuropatkin, whose armies had suffered at Lake Narotch, declared himself incapable of further offensive action until the autumn. Evert, on whom the main responsibility would fall, was dubious. Plainly he felt reluctant to expend his own resources in the preliminaries to an operation that would mainly reflect glory on a colleague. Brusilov, prompted by the Tsar's equivocation, changed his tack. He suggested that the main thrust should come from Evert, and be delivered after his own South-Western Front had shattered Conrad and drawn the German reserves south. Perhaps he calculated that, if the timing was close enough, Evert would be in time to distract German attention even if it meant that his own attack, now relegated to secondary status, would get a smaller allocation of resources.

Finally, the Tsar agreed and Evert, more reluctantly, appeared to do likewise. Brusilov returned to his HQ determined that, for once, a Russian operation would be perfectly prepared. To the individual army commanders Brusilov emphasised that the breakthrough had to be immediate. Too often in the past the drawn-out frontal battles had remained undecided until the Russian infantry were already dead on their feet from exhaustion and the artillery magazines empty. Relief models and even full-scale reproductions were built of all the important Austrian defence works which were carefully photographed by Russian pilots in the early part of May. All the assault units were carefully rehearsed in manoeuvres, the lessons discussed, the manoeuvres repeated. Brusilov was allocated no reserves, so no unusual rail traffic or newly identified prisoners could betray his plans. The artillery conserved their ammunition by firing only ranging shots for six weeks. Brusilov also risked making himself unpopular at St Petersburg by banishing a number of journalists and other hangers-on – court emissaries, business touts, and so forth – from his own HQ, and ordering his army commanders to do the same. Such an aversion to publicity, unprecedented in a senior general, was a measure of his determination.

Yet ultimately the success of the Russian summer offensive had to depend on Evert. As the hour approached the commander of the West Front dragged his feet ever more reluctantly. It had originally been postulated that Evert was to follow Brusilov at an interval of five days – the time taken for the German Army Group reserve to be committed. Brusilov, originally programmed to lead off on 29th May, was held back because Evert, apprehensive of tackling the Germans, 'could not give a date'. Brusilov's whole tactic depended on staggered offensives –

46   As preparations for the offensive reach their climax, Russian troops attend a service
in the field: now it was do or die

Tannenberg had shown that even a week's difference in timing could be fatal. Then came another desperate appeal from Paris. On top of the critical plight of the Verdun defenders (Fort Vaux was beleaguered and about to fall) bad tidings arrived from Italy where Conrad's picked divisions, fresh from quiet Galicia, had routed two Italian armies at Trentino.

Once again, and for the last time, the Tsar did as his allies asked. Brusilov was ordered to start his offensive; Evert was to follow as soon as possible. It was hoped (though not, it seems, on the strength of any particular assurance from Evert) that this would be on 9th June.

A BRILLIANT OPENING

On 4th June Brusilov attacked the Austrian positions, using all four armies simultaneously on a broad front and with no reserves above divisional strength. Although in complete defiance of conventional offensive doctrine, the attack succeeded brilliantly. By the evening of the first day the three Austrian defence lines which had been laid out in depth, a mile between each, had given way and in many places the white-bloused Russian infantry had broken into open, unscarred country. Mass desertions by Slav units in the Austrian army had eased their path and helped them, also, to overrun large stocks of food and ammunition.

47   Austrian Hussars surround a fire

48   Shell for 305 Austrian gun on a trolley

Within a week Austrian resistance had effectively vanished along a front almost 200 miles in length. Only a few German formations – General Bothmer's *Sudarmee*, and the two corps under the command of General Linsingen covering Ludendorff's right flank at Kovel – held against the tide, scraping together such battered Austrian remnants as were in their vicinity. For some days it was only on rocks such as these that the enemy position in the whole of south Poland depended – small groups of men, sometimes with a battery of 77-mm field-guns, at road and rail junctions, a few armoured trains, packets of dismounted cavalry, and desperate machine-gunners in the upper floors of village houses. At night they gained a brief respite, but during the long June days the probing Russian columns would search them out, draw fire, halt, unlimber their guns, advance again through the dust and smoke. Fighting a score or so of such actions each day, the four field armies tramped their way across the Galician plain, towards the Carpathians and the very centre of the Habsburg Empire.

Failure to support Brusilov cost Russia her last chance of victory and so lengthened the war

The German response was as Brusilov had predicted. Army Group Reserve, all five divisions, was sent south at once and placed under Conrad's command. (At the same time Ludendorff was protesting violently that *Oberost* should be given supreme command of the whole Eastern Front.) Conrad also reduced the scale of the operations in Italy so as to be able to use his only remaining reliable force in the East. Falkenhayn at once ordered four divisions away from the West Front in order to replenish Army Group Reserve.

Strategically then, Brusilov's offensive had already achieved its secondary objectives. But the pace of the advancing infantry was slackening; confusion, with 350,000 prisoners congesting the rear, began to multiply and STAVKA, excited by the scale of Brusilov's success, had taken to interfering almost daily and issuing orders direct to the individual army commanders. The moment for Evert to attack and thus sustain momentum had come – it was indeed almost past. On 9th June, at the five-day interval, Evert had announced himself unable to proceed until the 18th. The critical days dragged by with the strength, particularly the German strength, against Brusilov slowly accumulating as surely as it drained away from the front facing Evert. The 18th June came, and passed, and still there was no move. Evert had nearly 2,000,000 men standing still while Ludendorff (according to his own account written after the war) was down to a cavalry brigade and a few machine-gun units as his last reserve for the entire Front. When finally Evert went into action it was little more than a demonstration, being neither on the site, nor on the scale, agreed at the April conference. At the same time the STAVKA informed Brusilov that they would be reinforcing him strongly from the West Front ' . . . as he could make better use of them'.

This was a strategic blunder of the first order. However incompetently conducted, Evert's offensive must have had the effect of drawing the German reserves northward again, to bar the direct route across Poland into Silesia. The British attack on the Somme would ensure, for some weeks at least, that no more divisions were sent eastward out of France. The Russian approach was being watched with anxiety in the Balkans, particularly in Rumania, whose leaders were anxious to jump on the Allied bandwagon once their victory seemed certain (if only to avoid being penalised at the peace conference). The double blow of a Rumanian declaration of war on their southern flank and the collapse of their army in the field would undoubtedly have forced the Habsburgs to make peace and thereby, very probably, the Hohenzollerns also.

49　South-western front, war prisoners

50　Russian wounded

In point of fact Brusilov's reinforcements arrived very much more slowly (as he had foreseen) than the speed with which the enemy front, daily strengthened by German intervention, hardened against him. Obediently, as the new divisions arrived, Brusilov pressed forward against ever stiffening and more professionally directed resistance. Through the stifling heat of August the fighting dragged on, with Russian casualties creeping up now towards the 500,000 mark. By the end of the month even the STAVKA could see the futility of further attacks and the operation was called off, having gained enormous tracts of territory and the diversion of thirty-five German divisions from the West. Too late, the Rumanians finally declared war – a menace which no longer had substance once Brusilov had been halted. After some early success they were trampled to death by a German army under Mackensen and the Allies' position was worse than when Rumania had been neutral, for the STAVKA flank had to be extended to the Black Sea and German communications with Turkey were improved.

There was never at any time a possibility of winning the war on the Western Front (although there was a likelihood three times of losing it there). It was in the East, where the German General Staff had all along apprehended mortal danger, that the Allies generated, and discarded, their greatest opportunities: in 1914, when the victories in Galicia were annulled by defeat at Tannenberg, in 1915, when hesitation blighted the attack on the Dardanelles, and finally in 1916 with the Brusilov failure.

The Brusilov offensive was the last throw, the last grand gesture of the Imperial Russian Army. Had this operation been properly supported in its opening weeks the political collapse of Austria-Hungary would inevitably have followed the loss of her army in the field; a negotiated settlement with Germany would have brought peace to Europe while the old social order was still in control of diplomacy and politics. Whether this would have been a good or a bad thing is a judgement outside the scope of this work, but undeniably our history over the last fifty years would have been totally different.

6

Kerensky: Revolution and Surrender

AFTER THE FAILURE of the Brusilov offensive the Russian army no longer offered any real threat to the Germans in the East. Starved of munitions and equipment, with its officer corps decimated, the most that could be demanded of it was that by intelligent use of space and depth it might tie down any further enemy attacks.

In point of fact the German High Command had no intention of following what they saw as the mistakes of Napoleon, and a stalemate developed:

> The staff of the 10th Army was quartered in the small historic town of Iziaslavl. Its members did not appear to be greatly worried. Some of the officers were quite intelligent and all of them were most hospitable. After lunch, many of them would take a nap, and then spend the afternoon in a leisurely manner: some read novels under shady trees, others went off on their horses, a few practised acrobatics on a bicycle in the courtyard (!), while still others were playing *gorodki*, throwing heavy sticks at others planted at some distance. . . .
>
> Supper time was thus reached in a pleasant manner, and after the meal the officers sang. After the songs they went for a walk.
>
> The desk work consisted of two telegrams which Barychnikov endeavoured to make as colourless as possible. They would not think of trying anything new or original. I told them tonight that the Western armies were giving names to their trenches, so as to make their location and use easier. 'Bah,' replied Barychnikov, 'this can be useful when you get stuck in one place, as is precisely the case on the Western Front!' 'It seems to me that you too have been stuck here for some months now. You have had plenty of time to classify your positions.' 'Yes, yes,' he answered in a somewhat condescending way, 'in France you have technique but here in Russia we use *tvortchestvo* [creative force].'

This account comes from the diary of a Frenchman, Professor Legras, who was attached to a Russian division in the field, and its story is well corroborated by other reports of this period. Despite the torpor evident from this report, however, the climate of opinion in the army, as in every

51   Kerensky taking the salute 1917. His attempt in 1917 to force the Russian army into an offensive proved disastrously misjudged

52   A Russian officer using a field telephone

other group in society, was being changed by sheer pressure of events. In 1915 statutory exemptions for university students from military service had been abolished. Now, as the students arrived to take their commissions having attended shortened, and somewhat radical, university courses for officers, the effects of this were becoming apparent. Paléologue records the following remark by a member of the Council of the Emperor: 'It's ridiculous! Our corps of officers is to be contaminated! All these students are nothing but revolutionary virus which will infect the army!' In the ranks, many of the new conscripts had been taken from industries which had grown with the war, and where union sentiment, and conspiracy, had been strong.

At the beginning of January 1917 General Krymov arrived from the Front and asked to be given an opportunity of unofficially acquainting the members of the Duma with the 'disastrous conditions at the Front

53   Russian troops entering the town of Bukovina in 1917

and the spirit of the army'. Mikhail Rodzianko, the president of the
Duma, recalls how

> . . . A large number of members of the Duma, the Council of the Empire,
> and the Special Council assembled at my flat. The gallant General's tale
> was listened to with profound emotion. His was a painful and grim
> confession. There could be no hope of victory until the government had
> changed its course, or given way to another which the army could
> trust . . . .
>
> The spirit of the army is such that the news of a coup d'état would be
> welcomed with joy. A revolution is imminent, and we at the Front feel it
> to be so. If you decide on such an extreme step, we will support you . . . .

Once the army began to crumble, there could be no hope for the
regime. For it was on military strength that, ultimately, the whole
repressive apparatus of Tsarism depended. The officers acquiesced in,
even encouraged, the idea of a revolution, not in any radical sense but
simply as a means to greater efficiency. But for the men it was different.
Exposed to a continuous stream of tracts, leaflets, word-of-mouth
conspiracy and rumour; chivvied and harangued by anarchists, socialists,
communists, half-baked liberals of every kind, they had gradually come
to question the old order, whose battles they were fighting, and glance
hopefully towards the new Utopia of comfort and equality which the

54   The arrest of the Generals, February 1917

revolution seemed to promise. The following extract is the text of a leaflet distributed in the line in March 1917, prior to the Kerensky offensive:

> Brothers! We beg you not to obey an order that is meant to destroy us. An offensive is planned. Take no part in it. Our old leaders have no authority now. Our officers want to make an end of us. They are the traitors. They are the internal enemy. They would like everything to be as before. You know well that all our generals have been put on reduced pay, and they want this revenge.
>
> We shall be thrown back when we reach the enemy's wire. We cannot break through. I have reconnoitred in the enemy lines and I know that there are ten rows of it, with machine-guns every 15 yards. It is useless to advance. If we do we shall be dead men, with nothing left to hold our front.
>
> Pass this on, brothers, and promptly write other letters of the same sort.

MUTINY FOLLOWS STRIKES

At the beginning of March a succession of bread riots in St Petersburg culminated in a strike at the giant Putilov metalworks, whose workers drifted about the streets adding to the disorder. On the 8th the police, attempting to disperse the crowds, caused over 300 casualties with rifle

55   The revolutionary outbreak in St Petersburg

and machine-gun fire, but this merely exacerbated the confusion, and during the night many buildings in the heart of the capital were set on fire by the rioters. The police had lost control, only the army could restore order. But on the third day oft the riots the garrison mutinied and even the Cossacks, Tsarism's traditional instrument of repression, refused to ride against the mob.

From that time on the snowball of defections, strikes, and violence accumulated at frightening speed. The Duma refused to obey an imperial decree ordering its dissolution, and on 12th March proclaimed a 'provisional government' containing a number of prominent Liberals and Socialists, under the chairman of the County Councils. Every clandestine and subversive organisation – inside the army as much as among the workers – could now openly prosecute its aims without fear of the police, while soldiers roamed the streets in bands looking for officers and policemen and shooting on sight.

Nonetheless, at this stage the majority of people continued to pay lip-service to the need for continuing the war, and justified the revolution as a means to this end. General Danilov who, with General Ruzsky (victor of the first Galician campaign) actually secured the Tsar's resignation, had addressed him in the following form: 'Your Imperial Majesty, I am well aware of your profound love for our country. I am sure that to save it as well as the dynasty and in order to have the war prosecuted till victory, *you will consent to the sacrifice the war demands from you.* I don't see any other way, except the one expressed by the president of the Duma, and supported by my superiors in the army.' This was still a far cry from the peremptory order of the Soviet, for the arrest of 'Citizen Romanov'.

While chaos swept the army's rear areas, with barracks in mutiny, supply trains blocked, whole staffs of officers under close arrest, and orders issuing from *ex tempore* 'Military Soviets', the front line remained in atrophy:

> The parapet is crumbling away. No one troubles to repair it; no one feels inclined to do so, and there are not enough men in the company. There is a large number of deserters; more than fifty have been allowed to go. Old soldiers have been demobilised, others have gone on leave [sic] with the arbitrary permission of the Committee. Others, again, have been elected members of numerous committees, or gone away as delegates. Finally, by threats and violence, the soldiers have so terrorised the regimental surgeons that the latter have been issuing medical certificates even to the thoroughly fit.

56   Russian deserters, including officers, trying to take over a train

In the trenches the hours pass slowly and wearily, in dullness and idleness. In one corner men are playing cards, in another a soldier returned from leave is lazily and listlessly telling a story. Along the trenches comes Lieutenant Albov, the Company Commander. He said to the group of soldiers, somewhat irresolutely and entreatingly: 'Comrades, get to work quickly. In three days we have not made a single trench to the firing line.'

The card players did not even look round; someone said in a low voice, 'All right.' The man reading the newspaper rose and reported, in a familiar manner, 'The Company does not want to dig, because that would be the preparation for an advance, and the Committee has resolved . . .'

A Dutch businessman, resident at that time in St Petersburg, has described how the streets were filled with groups of dismounted Cossacks waiting for orders – '*any* orders, they would have as gladly ridden against the mob as with them'. This attitude pervaded the army in the field, and is well illustrated by General Denikin's description of the sequel to the incident above:

> The Regimental Commander [suddenly appeared in the trench]. 'What the devil does this mean? The man on duty does not come forward. The men are not dressed. Filth and stench. What are you about, Lieutenant?'
> The grey-headed colonel cast a stern glance on the soldiers which involuntarily impressed them. They all rose to their feet. He glanced through a loophole and, starting back, asked furiously, 'What is that?'
> In the green field, among the barbed wire, a regular bazaar was going on. A group of Germans and some of our men were bartering vodka, tobacco, lard, bread. Some way off a German officer reclining on the grass – red-faced, sturdy, with an arrogant look on his face – carried on a conversation with a soldier named Soloveytchik; and, strange to say, the familiar and insolent Soloveytchik stood before the lieutenant respectfully.
> The colonel pushed the observer aside and, taking his rifle from him, put it through the loophole. A murmur was heard among those watching. They began to ask him not to shoot. One of them, in a low voice as if speaking to himself, remarked, 'This is provocation.' The colonel, crimson with fury, turned to him for a moment and shouted, 'Silence!'
> All grew silent and pressed towards the loophole. A shot was heard, and the German officer convulsively stretched himself out and was still; blood was running from his head. The haggling soldiers scattered. The colonel threw the rifle down, and muttering through his teeth, 'Scoundrels!' strode further along the trenches. The 'truce' was over.

A DISASTROUS MISCALCULATION

In May, Kerensky had himself promoted from Minister of Justice to Sukhomlinov's old post at the Ministry of War and, in pursuit of the authority which seemed to have ebbed so far from the provisional government, began to prepare a great new offensive. He appointed Brusilov as Commander-in-Chief of the army and ordered him to strike once again in that amphitheatre of earlier Russian triumphs – Galicia.

It was a disastrous miscalculation. Hungry, discontented, poorly equipped, the Russian army was but a shadow of the indomitable and tenacious steam-roller which had twice crushed the Austrians on that battlefield. Supplies were short or non-existent, support from the rear and

57   The collapse of Kerensky's offensive: a loyal NCO tries to force deserting soldiers to
go back to the front line

58   The Russian Revolution brought equality of a kind -- a woman's battalion at St
Petersburg 1917

the flanks often failed even to begin. The few 'loyal' units lurched about, cut up by the enemy crossfire, until within two weeks all the ground gained – and more – had been lost, and those few who had preserved their enthusiasm for the war were finally embittered.

For the rest of the summer, while the British tore their own army to pieces at Passchendaele, the Eastern Front remained shrouded in an uneasy calm. The Russians, effectively disengaged, gave ground whenever pressed, while behind them, in Moscow, St Petersburg, and the provincial capitals, chaos and violence seethed.

Kerensky had dismissed Brusilov. His successor, Kornilov, became increasingly restive at the deterioration of order at home. In September 1917 Kornilov turned his army inward, and marched on St Petersburg with the intention of disciplining the Soviet. This meant the end of the Eastern Front, even as a shadow (although in fact the Central powers kept over eighty divisions there until 1918). Kerensky took fright and mobilised the extreme radical elements to resist Kornilov, arming the workers and releasing Trotsky and others from gaol.

In fact it was unnecessary. Kornilov's army melted away, deserting, changing sides – in most cases simply drifting homeward. The only authority in the capital were the 'Red Guards', answerable to the Bolsheviks.

On 8th November Lenin read his *Decree on Peace* to the Soviet Congress. There was to be an immediate armistice. Peace was to be negotiated 'without indemnities or annexations'. As things turned out, the negotiations (at Brest-Litovsk) dragged on for months while the Russian plenipotentiaries harangued the assembly on revolutionary principles until the Germans lost patience and restarted hostilities. In March the Bolsheviks signed the final surrender.

The empires of Central Europe held together for another year. Nor, when their fall came, was it so catastrophic. In the high summer of 1918 both German and Habsburg armies were running at full tide in the West, swollen by the reinforcements which each had transferred from the extinct Russian Front. But neither was strong enough, either strategically, or even in a tactical sense, to overcome for more than a few days the

Following the November coup by the Bolsheviks, peace negotiations began at Brest-Litovsk. But they dragged on until the Germans mounted a further offensive which took them deep into Russia and forced the Bolsheviks to sign a surrender

59   Lenin addressing a rally

60   Russian troops in flight from the advancing German forces

advantages which were endemic to defence against walking infantry and tanks which could not exceed 7 mph.

The attacks ran down. There was a lull, while both adversaries gasped for breath. Then it was the turn, yet again, of the Allies to lurch forward. They too were reminded of the delaying power of even a thin chain of machine-guns when the British broke the Hindenburg Line at a cost of 140,000 men, and still were held up in open country by the German sharpshooters.

It must have seemed as if the Central powers could hold for ever, when an unexpected development in the Balkans started a chain reaction that brought them down within weeks. This was the offensive, by the small Franco-British force at Salonika, which broke out of the Bulgarian lines containing it and forced, within a fortnight, the Bulgarians to sue for an armistice which was signed on the 29th September.

For two or three days Ludendorff's nerve collapsed. Suffering from the cumulative strain of overwork and a slight stroke he instructed the government that they should sue for an immediate armistice as the Bulgarian defection ' . . . had fundamentally changed the situation in view of the attacks then being launched on the Western Front, as troops destined for the West have to be despatched to Bulgaria'.

Prince Max of Baden, a politician with liberal and pacific leanings, was forthwith summoned to be Chancellor and given his orders. In vain he pleaded for a breathing space, ' . . . eight, ten, even four days before I have to appeal to the enemy'. All Ludendorff could repeat was, 'I want to save my army'. Accordingly, on 4th October, the Germans addressed their appeal for an immediate armistice to President Wilson, and announced their acceptance of the 'Fourteen Points'.

In itself, this was adroit enough. It avoided direct intercourse with the British and French, who were in a bellicose and punitive frame of mind, and gave an illusory impression that Germany and the United States were now on the same side, idealistically trying to stop the war. Germany, with her liberal Chancellor and free press and Social Democrat cabinet had, overnight, become 'good'. But . . . *C'est le premier pas qui coûte*. Although the Front (as has been explained) was hardening and the Allied attacks dying down, the heady democratic atmosphere at home accelerated the disintegration of morale and discipline, just as the Tsar's machine had crumbled in Kerensky's hand. Riots, mutinies, open-air 'protest' rallies – this was the reality of the 'stab in the back'.

Meanwhile further blows rocked the Southern Front. Allenby entered

61   The Russian delegation arrives by train from St Petersburg for the peace conference at Brest-Litovsk, 24 February 1918

Damascus on the 1st October and the Turks fell back 350 miles in thirty-eight days. On 31st October they too capitulated. Now only the poor Habsburgs remained, with Germany in ferment to the north, and their southern *glacis* still further exposed by the collapse of Turkey. An Italian attack on Monte Grappa was heavily defeated. But when a small British force under Lord Cavan (sent out to 'stiffen' the Italian army after Caporetto) worked round their flank, the Austrians too, appealed to Wilson. This time, unfortunately, it was different. Wilson had promised independence to the Poles, and to the Czechs; he had also given 'assurances' to the Rumanians and the Slovenes. It was they, he replied, who must decide the peace terms. Immediately Austro-Hungary too disintegrated; the 'National Committees' which had for so long lain dormant sprang to life and demanded – usually without much bloodshed – their territorial birthright.

It was stalemate, rather than total defeat (as the Russians had been defeated) that had led to disorder within. These revolutions were mildly nationalistic, essentially bourgeois – not 'radical' in any sense. The hierarchic structure of society was toned down – not obliterated. The bourgeoisie were asserting themselves, and their new economic power, whose base had been so greatly broadened by the war. They wanted a larger say in the running of things, and nationalism and a kind of spurious democracy offered the easiest route to this end.

But in Russia, it had been very different. There the most autocratic and the most powerful country in the world had been laid low. Three times the Tsarist army had victory within its grasp – a victory that would have allowed the Russians to march at will across Europe, recasting its geography and perpetuating – perhaps indefinitely – its social order.

Now the very elements which had corroded that power and thwarted that victory had combined to produce a revolution as deep and as significant as that of 1789 in Paris. Militarily the country was powerless, as impotent as the feeblest Balkan principality. There was comfort only in the prophecy of the leader of 'National Liberation', Briantchaninov, made twenty-five years too soon:

> The only thing that can save this country now is a revolution. The revolution, as I see and desire it, would be a violent release of all the dynamic forces of the nation, a sublime resurrection of all Slav energies. After a few days of unavoidable troubles, perhaps even a month of disorder and paralysis, Russia would rise again with a grandeur you cannot imagine. Then you would see what the moral resources of the Russian nation are! It has inexhaustible reserves of courage, enthusiasm, and magnanimity. It's the greatest centre of idealism in the world!

62   Herr von Khulmann signing the treaty of Brest-Litovsk

63   Repairing a wire entanglement stockade

Chronology of Events

1914

7th August: Rennenkampf crosses the East Prussian frontier

10th August: Conrad begins his advance into Galicia

20th August: the Germans are defeated at Gumbinnen

26th–29th August: the Germans annihilate Samsonov's army at the battle of Tannenberg

1st–12th September: the Galician battles of Lemberg, Gródek, Rava-Russkaya, and Krasnik are fought

3rd October: the Germans take command of the centre and form their IX Army under Falkenhayn; they begin to invade Poland

10th–25th October: the Germans take Łódź and the battle of Warsaw is fought

29th October: Turkey enters the war

14th November: the Toruń operation is begun

13th–15th December: the Austrians are defeated in Serbia

1915

7th–14th February: a 'winter battle' is fought in Masuria and the Russians are ejected from East Prussia

22nd March: Przemyśl falls to the Russians and 126,000 prisoners are taken

28th April: Mackensen's offensive begins in West Galicia; the Russians give way at the battle of Gorlice-Tarnow

3rd June: Przemyśl is retaken by the Austro-German forces

22nd June: Lemberg falls

29th June: the German offensive is extended to central Poland

5th August: Ivangorod and Warsaw fall

25th August: Brest–Litovsk falls

5th September: the Tsar assumes the supreme command of the Russian Imperial Army

28th November: the Germans are defeated at Pinsk

1916

18th March–14th April: the battle of Lake Narotch is fought

4th April: Brusilov succeeds Ivanov as CO of the Southern Front

4th June: the Brusilov offensive opens

19th June: the Russians cross the River Pruth

10th July: the Brusilov offensive peters out. 300,000 Austrian prisoners are taken

27th August: Rumania enters the war on the side of the Allies

29th August: Falkenhayn is dismissed. Hindenburg and Ludendorff are appointed to the Western Front

October–November: Mackensen's campaign in Rumania

6th December: Bucharest falls

1917

11th March: food riots take place in Petrograd

12th–13th March: the Provisional Government is formed in Petrograd

15th March: the Tsar abdicates. British Labour leaders send a telegram of sympathy to the Russian Labour Party

16th May: Kerensky is appointed minister of war

1st July: the Brusilov/Kerensky offensive opens, but peters out on the 15th

2nd August: Brusilov and Kerensky resign

6th August: Kerensky appoints himself prime minister

25th–27th August: a 'National Conference' is held at Moscow; Kornilov appeals for 'measures to restore discipline'

3rd September: the Germans capture Riga

8th September: Kornilov marches on Petrograd

15th November: Kerensky flees and the Bolsheviks triumph

29th November: hostilities cease

2nd December: the Brest-Litovsk conference opens

15th December: an armistice agreement is signed

Author's Suggestions for Further Reading

THERE IS A dearth of short, general works that show the Eastern Front in its wider context. The two best are A.J.P. Taylor's *The First World War* (Hamish Hamilton) and B.H. Liddell Hart's *The War in Outline* (Faber).

On the German side all the participants (Ludendorff, Falkenhayn, Hindenburg, etc.) wrote memoirs or memoir forms. Incomparably the best – though still somewhat coloured in places by hindsight – are those of Major-General Max Hoffmann, *War Diaries and Other Papers* (two volumes, translated by Eric Sutton, 1929). Serious students will also find that, in addition to the plethora of personal reminiscence, it is possible to verify most facts from the German Official History, *Der Weltkrieg 1914–18* (fourteen volumes, published in Berlin between 1925 and 1944).

On the Russian side there is General Nicholas N. Golovine's *The Russian Campaign of 1914* (translated by A.C.S. Muntz, 1933). Golovine includes a number of official battle reports as, for instance, from Generals Martos and Potovsky. He also wrote a general history, *The Russian Army in the First World War* (Carnegie Endowment). General Basil Gourko wrote *Russia 1914–17, Memories and Impressions of War and Revolution* (New York, 1919).

Two foreigners inside Russia have given their accounts of events: Major-General Sir Alfred Knox in his book *With the Russian Army* (two volumes, 1921), and Maurice Paléologue, the French ambassador to St Petersburg, in *An Ambassador's Memoirs* (three volumes, translated by F.A. Holt, Hutchinson).

Index

Maps and illustrations are indicated by bold page numbers.

GREAT BATTLES SERIES

HASTINGS
Peter Poyntz Wright
Paperback £9.99 Illustrated

AGINCOURT
Christopher Hibbert
Paperback £9.99 Illustrated

EDGEHILL: 1642
Peter Young
Paperback £15.99 Illustrated

MARSTON MOOR: 1644
Peter Young
Paperback £15.99 Illustrated

THE BATTLE OF THE BOYNE AND AUGHRIM:
THE WAR OF THE TWO KINGS
John Kinross
Paperback £10.99 Illustrated

CORUNNA
Christopher Hibbert
Paperback £12.99 Illustrated

WELLINGTON'S PENINSULAR VICTORIES
Michael Glover
Paperback £12.99 Illustrated

TRAFALGAR: THE NELSON TOUCH
David Howarth
Paperback £10.99 Illustrated

BORODINO
Digby Smith
Paperback £12.99 Illustrated

WATERLOO: A NEAR RUN THING
David Howarth
Paperback £12.99 Illustrated

ARNHEM
Christopher Hibbert
Paperback £10.99 Illustrated

Order from THE WINDRUSH PRESS, LITTLE WINDOW, HIGH
STREET, MORETON-IN-MARSH, GLOS. GL56 0LL
MAJOR CREDIT CARDS ACCEPTED
TEL: 01608 652012 FAX: 01608 652125
Please add £1 post and packing within the UK

MILITARY HISTORY BOOKS

LETTERS HOME FROM THE CRIMEA
A young cavalryman's campaign
Edited by Philip Warner
Paperback £9.99

THE LETTERS OF PRIVATE WHEELER 1809–1828
An eyewitness account of the Battle of Waterloo
Edited and with a foreword by B. H. Liddell Hart
*'Vivid images – of people, landscape, events – flow from his pen . . .
one of military history's great originals'*
John Keegan
Paperback £9.99

THE DIARY OF A NAPOLEONIC FOOT SOLDIER
Jakob Walter
A conscript in the *Grande Armée*'s account of the long march home on the
retreat from Moscow
Edited and Introduced by Marc Raeff
Paperback £9.99 Illustrated

THE RECOLLECTIONS OF RIFLEMAN HARRIS
One of the most popular military books of all time
Edited and Introduced by Christopher Hibbert
*'An ordinary soldier's memoirs are rare but precious. Harris's are a most
vivid record of the war in Spain and Portugal against Napoleon, the same campaign
as featured in the recent TV drama series, 'Sharpe'.'*
The Mail on Sunday
Paperback £9.99

THE RECOLLECTIONS OF SERGEANT MORRIS
These are among the liveliest and most revealing of that remarkable series of
memoirs left by soldiers who fought against Napoleon
Edited by John Selby with an introduction by Peter Young
Paperback £9.99

A SOLDIER OF THE SEVENTY-FIRST
The journal of a Soldier in the Peninsular War
Edited and Introduced by Christopher Hibbert
'His elegant style and his descriptive power take us with him at every step.'
The Sunday Telegraph
Paperback £9.99

THE WHEATLEY DIARY
A Journal & Sketchbook from the Peninsular War &
The Waterloo Campaign
Edited and Introduced by Christopher Hibbert
Paperback £10.99 Illustrated in colour